Offenders in Transition:
Just Trying to Do Good

also by Lee Streetman

Drugs, Delinquency, and Pregnancy,
a Panel Study of Adolescent Problem Behaviors

Streetman Soldiers in the War of the Rebellion,
Civil War-era documents

The Relationship of Delinquent Behavior
and Alcohol/Drug Involvement to Adolescent
Nonmarital Pregnancy and its Resolution

Offenders in Transition:
Just Trying to Do Good

an Assessment of
Health Risks and Concerns

Lee G. Streetman, Ph.D.

iUniverse, Inc.
New York Lincoln Shanghai

Offenders in Transition: Just Trying to Do Good
an Assessment of Health Risks and Concerns

iUniverse books may be ordered through booksellers or by contacting:

iUniverse
2021 Pine Lake Road, Suite 100
Lincoln, NE 68512
www.iuniverse.com
1-800-Authors (1-800-288-4677)

Because of the dynamic nature of the Internet, any Web addresses or links contained in this book may have changed since publication and may no longer be valid.

ISBN: 978-0-595-46001-4 (pbk)
ISBN: 978-0-595-90301-6 (ebk)

Printed in the United States of America

Contents

List of Tables

Acknowledgments

This research was funded by NIMH grant R03MH62968 in response to Program Announcement (PAR-99-140) NIMH Small Grants Program. I wish to thank Dr. Judith Rabkin of Columbia University. I also wish to thank Willo Pequegnat, Rick Wiese, David Stoff, and Chris Gordon of The National Institute of Mental Health. In addition, I appreciate the assistance of Jim Deel and Dan Widener of the Delaware Department of Corrections and Alfred Onuonga of the Delaware Center for Justice. I wish to acknowledge the Delaware HIV Consortium and AIDS Delaware for their valuable assistance. Thanks to my friends and family members who put up with me during the stressful moments that typically accompany primary research. Finally, I want to acknowledge the interview subjects of this study. Thank you all for your valuable contributions to our understanding of offender release and reentry.

Foreword

All research begins somewhere. I am a sociologist and an educator who strongly believes that helping others is a worthwhile endeavor. This is how I became interested in studying the health risks and concerns among released offenders who were trying their best to make it on the outside.

My father was a manager at a chemical company which frequently transferred us to different parts of the country. I disliked the transition and being uprooted so often while I was growing up, but I enjoyed traveling and soon noticed the differences in the way individuals talked and acted in Texas, Oklahoma, Idaho, Louisiana, New Jersey, Illinois, West Virginia, Iowa, Pennsylvania, and Delaware. After graduating high school I joined the Marine Corps and journeyed to South Carolina, North Carolina, Virginia, California and then overseas to places such as Iwakuni, Japan. My military experience further exposed me to the diversity of individual backgrounds. Because of these early life experiences I became interested in studying human behavior. Following my discharge I enrolled in college. I tried several majors before deciding that I wanted to know more about the influence of groups on our behavior. Therefore, I studied sociology.

Sociology is a systematic examination of group behavior, how individuals affect groups, how groups affect individuals, and how groups affect each other. I was interested in how being a member of a group influences conformity to the various rules that guide our behavior. I was drawn to the myriad ways groups respond and sanction those who deviate from these normative expectations. Finally, I was interested in how individuals and groups attempt to correct problems in society.

In graduate school I concentrated in the area of deviance and criminology. During this time I began to research the effects of disruptions in the lifecourse. This research examined the consequences of early childbearing among females. My data consisted of interviews with 93 young women who were participating in state-sponsored training programs, many of whom were unwed mothers. One explanation for early unwed childbearing was that the females who got pregnant had lower self-esteem than those who did not get pregnant. However, my research showed that there was much variation in measures of self-esteem among the sample groups. Those who had higher self-esteem were employed. This study also revealed the symbolic importance of motherhood as a passage into adult status. The intervening effects of normative group anchorage exerted a mediating effect between cognitive ability and self-esteem. In other words, self-esteem is mediated through social interaction and group membership. It is not a direct result of cognitive abilities.

These findings illustrate one of the allures of sociological inquiry. Through systematic research we discover that what many people think "makes sense" is actually due to other factors. The effect of group anchorage, such as having a job, was a powerful source of positive self-esteem. Who we are and how we identify ourselves is largely a product of cultural and subcultural influences. We know that culture has a major impact on who we are. But the specific socialization experiences resulting from our gender, race and ethnicity, family, peers, schools, neighborhood, occupation, religion, region, and so on, also affects our beliefs, values, and actions. Therefore, as we grow up each of these factors influences us by providing a pattern of guidelines, or what we refer to as an age-graded normative structure.

What is expected of us depends to a large degree on our age and the normative structure of the groups making judgements. I continued to research early childbearing, examining several long-term consequences. This research compared the educational and financial outcomes in early adulthood of 6,074 men and women. The analysis utilized a sophisticated statistical model that controlled for the background factors of race, ethnicity, and family socioeconomic status. Results showed that the educational and financial outcomes varied significantly depending on the occurrence of a nonmarital adolescent pregnancy, the resolution of nonmarital adolescent pregnancy, and the age at which adolescent pregnancy occurs. For both males and females, those who started families earlier were "penalized" with lower levels of educational and financial attainment over their life-course.

In *Drugs, Delinquency, and Pregnancy*, I examined the development of "problem behaviors" among a group of 7,727 teenagers. Specifically, I looked at how early experiences with delinquency, drugs and alcohol, and being involved in a teen pregnancy, could escalate in later adolescence and young adulthood. Consistent with previous juvenile delinquency research, the earlier an individual became involved in these behaviors the more likely he or she would continue over the lifecourse. Several psychosocial indicators, such as cynicism, self-derogation, powerlessness, family stress, school stress, peer rejection, and peer delinquency, were hypothesized to mediate the effects of background characteristics on the frequency and intensity of problems behaviors. But contrary to earlier research, many adolescents "specialized" in one form of problem behavior, fewer were involved in two or more.

While working on this research I began tutoring juveniles who had been adjudicated delinquent. I volunteered with a Junior Achievement project in a juvenile detention facility and began teaching adult prison inmates the "Thresholds" program that helps individuals improve their decision-making skills. This volunteer work provided me with the opportunity to interact with offenders and to see life inside prison.

People are fascinated with jails and prisons. Today, television programs like "Lock Up" are popular. Several former penitentiaries have reopened as tourist attractions, including Eastern State Penitentiary in Philadelphia, Alcatraz in San Francisco, and the West Virginia State Penitentiary in Moundsville. But interviewing offenders about their transition to life outside is just recently being subjected to systematic study.

As the Research Specialist for the Delaware Council on Crime and Justice I collected data at all of the juvenile and adult corrections facilities in Delaware and a few in Maryland. I was the program evaluator for an AIDS/HIV education project. It was here that I discovered the differential risks that incarcerated populations face with diseases such as HIV/AIDS.

Using the U.S. Department of Justice's Bureau of Justice Statistics data I discovered a significant correlation between state incarceration rates and rates of HIV/AIDS. Then using data from UNAIDS and from the International Centre for Prison Studies, I showed a similar significant correlation between these rates at national and international levels. I presented this research at the annual meetings of the Global Awareness Society International in Accra, Ghana. As a result of this work I was invited to do further research at the distinguished International Centre for Prison Studies at Kings College School of Law at the University of London.

I worked with the Prevention Committee of the Delaware HIV Consortium and in 2001, I submitted a proposal to The National Institutes of Health. I received a grant award from the National Institute of Mental Health to assess health risks among inmates who were scheduled to be released. This book presents the findings of this seminal study.

Preface

Offenders in Transition explores how individuals adjust to the release and reentry experience following incarceration. This research analyzes data collected from interviews with offenders during the transition period from prison and return back to neighborhoods and communities in an effort to better understand the decision-making processes involved in HIV/AIDS risk reduction. Specifically, why do some offenders, despite knowing about and intending to avoid HIV/AIDS risks, continue to engage in risky behavior following their release from prison?

Jails and prisons are places of physical, psychological, and social transition. They are sites of continuous entry, detention, exit, and re-incarceration for many persons who are disproportionately disadvantaged members of the community. Incarceration heightens marginalization, especially in an era where prisons and what happens inside them are increasingly removed from public awareness. Risk behaviors that result in incarceration, risk behaviors that occur during incarceration, and risk behaviors that offenders take during the release/reentry transition pose health threats to the communities which receive released offenders, many of whom may not know their HIV status.

Social and economic changes in wider society affect the internal dynamics of correctional facilities and the health characteristics of prisoner admissions. In addition to pronounced HIV rates among prison entrants, HIV transmission within prisons is greater where inmates serve longer terms and where inmates have histories of prior drug use. Overcrowding and unacceptable staff-to-inmate ratios contribute to incidents of interpersonal violence, and compound other behaviors such as unprotected sexual activity, drug use, and unsterile tattooing/body piercing that pose serious health risks for inmates. Therefore, the well-being of communities is affected when offenders are released.

First, the relationship between offender release/reentry and HIV/AIDS is introduced. Next, the correlation between HIV/AIDS and incarceration rates is examined followed by a discussion of the research methodology. Then Chapter Four presents interviews with inmates prior to their release, followed by a discussion of the post-release interviews of male and female offenders. Chapter Six analyzes the decision-making processes of offenders. Specifically, the pre-release behavioral intention of inmates is contrasted with their actual behaviors during the release/reentry transition. Finally, the results are discussed with suggestions for further research.

1

Introduction

Reasons for the commission of crime have long roots in American culture, and over the centuries a variety of measures have been used to keep citizens in line. In the early days of eighteenth-century corrections, inmates were believed to be flawed by their absence of spirituality. The nineteenth century defined flaw as offenders' absence of employability. Inmate labor was exploited and rationalized as a mechanism to enhance felons' vocational knowledge, skills, and abilities. That theme of enhancing vocational skills has persisted into the twenty-first century (Krienert and Fleisher 2004:42).

Corrections has undergone many transformations since John Howard sought reform of Bridewells. Other reformers including Maconochie, Crofton, and Fry deserve credit for their efforts to humanize incarceration. Yet the idea of corrections as a form of rehabilitation seems to have floated down the river, replaced by a neo-Code of Draco to deal with wrongdoing.

This chapter will outline why offenders being released from incarceration is an important area of study. An examination of rates of incarceration and the characteristics of those incarcerated reveals that they share some of the same correlates with rates of HIV/AIDS and the characteristics of those affected. Moreover, a key concept for understanding offenders in transition is *transience*.

The root of both transition and transience is "trans" which means to pass or cross through, over, or beyond. Transition literally refers to a passing away with time, not permanent, or being temporary. So "transitory" is that which by its inherent nature must sooner or later pass or end. Due to this inherent quality of passing or "placelessness," transience engenders marginality.

Marginality is the partial assimilation of the values, beliefs, and norms of more than one group simultaneously. As a feeling of transition, most people find a state of marginality uneasy because the normative structure of the former group is different from that of the new group. Finding yourself as a new person in the group, whether it be a classroom, military unit, a correctional facility, or neighborhood, can be stressful because the new group expectations are not clearly defined.

Transience and marginality may be accompanied by feelings of isolation, powerlessness, and alienation. It may precipitate a careless state of mind. And in some situations, perhaps at critical periods during the day or night, individuals may disregard the consequences of risk behaviors, particularly in harsh "total institutions" such as jails and prisons (Foreman 2003; Schmid and Jones 1996; Streetman 1996). Marginality is not confined to offenders; family and friends who regularly visited inmates may suddenly discontinue as an example of the "transition anxiety" that typically precedes the weeks just prior to release from prison.

Therefore, the transition to prison, the transitory nature of incarceration, and particularly the transition from prison and back to family and community are important areas of consideration when examining risk-taking behaviors. In Delaware, prison officials do not routinely test for infection unless they are aware of an inmate's illness prior to arrival, or if symptoms arise during incarceration. Importantly, about 97% of Delaware's inmates (including those with HIV) will be released back into the community and almost 60% will reenter within five years (Delaware Statistical Analysis Center 2006).

Rates of incarceration are correlated with health risks such as HIV/AIDS at state, national, and international levels (Streetman 2002). HIV/AIDS infection rates among the nation's incarcerated populations vary by offense category and are linked to the proportion of offenders with a history of injecting drug use (IDU) and to the rate of HIV infection among injecting drug users in the community (Hammett, Harmon, and Maruschak 1999). IDUs are over-represented in jails and prisons; facilities with the highest HIV rates are located where HIV infection in the community is widespread among IDUs (Jurgens 1999). According to the Office of AIDS Research, about 83% of intravenous drug users have been in jail or prison.

Several surveillance systems provide estimates of the incidence and prevalence of infection, morbidity, and mortality from HIV/AIDS in the U.S. population. The Centers for Disease Control and Prevention reports that 14.7 persons per 100,000 population in the U.S. are infected with HIV/AIDS. According to the CDC, men who have sex with men (MSM) remains a high risk group for HIV infection in the US. The highest HIV infection prevalence rates among populations at risk for HIV nationwide were found among MSM who sought treatment at sexually transmitted disease (STD) clinics. The median prevalence rate was 19.3%. MSM also comprise the largest proportion (60%) of men diagnosed with AIDS. Among women tested in STD clinics, HIV prevalence varies in a pattern that reflects the prevalence rates among injecting drug users (IDUs).

CDC data also shows that the HIV/AIDS prevalence among IDUs varies by geographic region. The highest prevalence rates in surveyed drug treatment centers were in the Northeast, the South, and Puerto Rico. IDUs diagnosed with AIDS represented 24% of AIDS cases in men and 47% of those in women. The disproportionate impact of HIV/AIDS on racial/ethnic minority populations has been demonstrated in most surveys. HIV prevalence is higher in non-Hispanic blacks than in other racial/ethnic groups. Non-Hispanic blacks accounted for 47%, and Hispanics 20%, of persons diagnosed with AIDS (CDC 2005).

The CDC reports that AIDS remains the leading killer of young African-American men and the second leading killer of young African-American women. Comprising only 13 percent of the U.S. population, African-Americans account for 57 percent of the new infections and African-Americans and Latinos make up 82 percent of HIV positive women aged 13-24. African-American women are eight times more likely to contract HIV than white women and their odds of infection are three times higher than those of Latinos. Researchers point to the risks of unprotected sex with men who may hide their intravenous drug use or bisexual encounters (see National Library of Medicine 1994; NIH 1995, 1997; Tillman and Pequegnat 1997).

According to the Delaware Department of Health and Social Services (2005), those aged 30-39 account for 46% of Delaware's HIV/AIDS cases followed by ages 40-49 (29%), and ages 20-29 (14%). The overall exposure category and transmission mode show that injecting drug use (IDU) accounts for almost 42% of HIV cases in the state, followed by men who have sex with men (MSM) at 31% and 19% from heterosexual contact.

HIV/AIDS INSIDE INCARCERATION FACILITIES

Less examined is the differential impact of the penal system on African-Americans, where AIDS infection is six times higher, as a source of the growing infection rates of African-American women (CDC 1998; MMWR 1992, 1996; Office of AIDS Research 1997). With one out of three adult African-American males either in prison, on probation or parole (BJS 2006), the possibility of HIV exposure and potential crossover is alarming.

In addition to pronounced HIV rates among prison entrants, HIV transmission within prisons is greater where inmates serve longer terms. Unacceptable staff-to-inmate ratios contribute to incidents of interpersonal violence, and compound other behaviors such as drug use, unprotected sexual activity, and unsterile tattooing/body piercing (Baker, Doe, Epstein, Hagans, Siers, Streetman, and Woodlin 2001; Braithwaite, Hammett, and Mayberry 1996; CDC 2005, 2006; Hammett et al. 1999; Laszlo and Smith 1991). Overcrowding in jails and prisons is a prominent factor in disease transmission and documented cases of custodial seroconversion (Jurgens 1999; Malkin and Elliot 1995; Marquart, Merianos, Herbert, and Carroll 1997; Schedffer and Marthe 2000).

According to the Survey of Inmates in State and Federal correctional facilities (1991–97), the rise in state prison population is partly the result of the increasing numbers of parole violators returned to prison. Of those returned to prison, 60% were arrested/convicted of a new offense. The rate of release declined from 37 per 100 state prisoners in 1990 to 31 per 100 in 1998. The average time served among first releases increased from 22 months (1990) to 28 months (1998). Overall, the largest growth in state inmates between 1990-98 was among violent offenders (229,300, or 51% of the growth), while the number of drug offenders grew 87,100 (19% of the growth), property offenders (15%) and public-order offenders (15%). Drug offenses comprise the largest group (58%) of Federal inmates sentenced in 1998. According to the Bureau of Justice Statistics (2006), new court commitments increased by 18% since 1998.

HIV infection rates also vary by offense category and drug history (Maruschak 1999). Inmates sentenced on a drug offense in state prisons have the highest rate (2.9%). Of property offenders, 2.4% test HIV positive. Rates are lower for violent and public-order offenders (1.9% each). Of state prison inmates who reported never using drugs, 1.7% test positive for HIV. An estimated 2.3% of inmates who had ever used drugs are HIV positive, other HIV positive rates include 2.7% of those who used drugs in the month before their current offense, 4.6% of those who had used a needle to inject drugs, and 7.7% of those who had shared a needle.

The rate of confirmed AIDS in prison (55 per 10,000 inmates) was at least 5 times the rate in the US general population (10 per 10,000 US residents age 13 or older). The HIV-positive inmates were concentrated in the state prisons of New York (7,500) and Florida (2,325) which held more than 40% of all HIV-infected inmates. In addition, 3.5% of all female state prison inmates were HIV positive, compared to 2.2% of male state prisoners (Maruschak 1999).

Black women in federal prisons were six times as likely to be HIV positive as white women. State inmates age 35-44 had the highest rates of infection (3.1%), whereas those age 24 or younger had the lowest (.5%) rate. In state prisons 26% of HIV-positive inmates had AIDS, in federal prisons, 36% (Maruschak 1999). At the end of 1997 23,548 inmates were infected with HIV, with 538 deaths due to AIDS. The rate of death due to AIDS was 48 deaths per 100,000 inmates. Between 1991 and 1996 about one in three state prisoner deaths were attributable to AIDS, however, during 1997 it was about one in five.

Fortunately, correctional facilities have become optimal settings for the development, delivery, and study of AIDS education and prevention programs (Ace Program 1998; Carney, Werth, and Morris 1997; Comfort, Grinstead, Faigeles, and Zack 2000; Grinstead, Zack, Faigeles, Grossman, and Blea 1999a; Kalichman 1998; Mantell, DiVittis, and Auerback 1997; Martin, Zimmerman, and Long 1993; Martin, Zimmerman, Long, and West 1995; Stevens 1993). The next chapter takes a broader look at the relationship between rates of HIV/AIDS and incarceration rates.

2

Correlation of HIV/AIDS & Incarceration Rates

Imagine a place where "adult prisoners put in orders for boys" and juveniles are smuggled into adult facilities and "rented out for short-time sex" over a period of several months. This is what Jolofani and DeGabriele (2002) discovered in their study of the Zomba, Blantyre, and Lilongwe Prisons in Malawi. One prisoner told the researchers that "some men have up to three *wives*" and "these boys have been in our cells for over six months." Additionally, the overcrowded conditions and the lack of food and medical attention have contributed to a dire situation. An overview of the global condition may offer insights into our present situation in the United States and a thorough look at the health risk decision-making among offender populations can reveal important insights into HIV/AIDS prevention (Okigbo, Okigbo, Hall, and Ziegler 2002; Streetman 2002).

According to ICPS Director Andrew Coyle,

> It is true that some prisoners are dangerous and a threat to the public but in all prison systems these make up a small proportion of the total. The reality is that if one visits prisons in most countries one can see the sections of society which are marginalised: ethnic minorities, the poor, the mentally ill, the unemployed and the homeless. (ICPS 2000).

The *2006 AIDS Epidemic Update* shows that there were 2.9 million AIDS deaths in 2006 and that 4.3 million people were newly infected with HIV in 2006. Estimates of the prevalence of HIV/AIDs in prison reveal that the rate may be 10 times higher than that among members of the general population according to UNAIDS/WHO. Incarceration offers optimal conditions for the spread of HIV such as injecting drug use (IDU), sexual tension, tatooing, and a general climate of violence and fear.

Three countries (the United States, China, and Russia) incarcerate about half of the world's 9 million prisoners (Walmsley 2006). Huge variations in incarceration rates exist between countries and reliable data is difficult to collect. Some regions refuse to open their doors to outsiders.[1] Moreover, funding for such projects is severely lacking. The International Centre for Prison Studies (ICPS) reported that some of the most problematic prison systems in the world include Russia, Turkey, Venezuela, Kazakstan, and Brazil. A sampling of the grave situations around the world follows, however, this is by no means an exhaustive account.

The ICPS maintains that the physical conditions in Russian prisons are among the worst, with "three prisoners often sharing one bed and living with continuous likelihood of contracting contagious diseases." The Itar Wire Service reported that Russian prisons have about 1,900 HIV-infected in the county's prisons, primarily in the Rostov and Kaliningrad regions according to Russia's chief of Justice Ministry's penitentiary department, Vladimir Yalunin.

As of May 2000, there were 25 known cases of HIV infection in the prisons of Azerbaijan, some 4,000 prisoners have been tested in the past two years. The head of the Russian Centre for the prevention of AIDS predicted that the number of AIDS cases in Russia would reach 1 million within two years. He claimed that only one fifth of all HIV cases were officially registered, and as many as 80% of HIV-infected people were between 15-25 years old.

1.　After presenting a paper on international rates of incarceration and HIV/AIDS at a 2001 global conference in Ghana, I attempted to tour a prison in Accra. Authorities refused my request.

Ukraine officials proposed isolating HIV-infected prisoners in separate facilities, saying that about 2,100 prisoners are infected, some 70% of whom are male. Pending governmental approval, HIV positive inmates would be moved to two existing jails staffed by doctors and nurses trained in HIV care. In Turkey, violent confrontations between staff and inmates are common. A lack of proper management contributes to levels of corruption and violence that put Venezuela prisons among the world's worst. Levels of tuberculosis in Kazakstan are as high as 20%.

Prisons in Brazil have witnessed violent deaths recently. However, epidemiologists at the University of Campinas reported that AIDS is the leading cause of death in Brazilian prisons. Twenty-one of 25 deaths registered at the prison hospital in Porto Alegre Prison, resulted from AIDS. Research showed that 17.3% of the detainees in Carandiru tested positive for HIV, at Sao Paulo, the rate was 12.5%. The prevalence of HIV in Brazil's prisons is about 15% according to the Health Ministry.

Official figures in Brazil show that out of a population of 175 million, approximately 150,000 men and women are incarcerated. A study of state prisons in Rio de Janeiro discovered that 25% of Brazilians living with HIV are infected by sharing needles. Injecting drug users were less likely to use condoms and had more risk factors than non IDUs. Men were more likely to share needles inside prison, whereas women more likely to share needles outside of prison.

Extreme human rights abuses confront HIV positive inmates in Uruguay, including stigmatization, a lack of harm reduction, and a lack of medical and social supports.

Canada's first national HIV/AIDS and Prisons Workshop was organized by the Toronto-based Prisoners with HIV/AIDS Support Action Network (PASAN). They charged that infected inmates do not receive the care, support, and treatment that would be available to them on the outside. According to PASAN, most people do not consider prisons as part of the community. In Canada rates of HIV infection vary between one and 7.2%; most correctional systems have rates under 1%, but countries in southern Europe report extremely high rates (Jurgens 1999; UNAIDS 2006).

Reporting on the situation of HIV/AIDS and tuberculosis in European prisons, a joint UNAIDS/WHO European seminar maintained that the rate of HIV and TB among prison populations are at levels many times higher than those in the general population. More than one-fifth of the prison population is HIV positive in some countries. Because TB is airborne, overcrowded prisons provide optimal conditions for transmission between prisoners, staff, and visitors.

A study of 9 of the 15 prisons in Ireland found that 37% of the inmates were infected with hepatitis C, 9% with hepatitis B, and 2% tested positive for HIV. Higher rates were reported among IDUs (21% claimed that they began injecting drugs *after* they were incarcerated).

Evidence of HIV transmission occurring in prisons was discovered in Scotland and in two Australian prisons in the early 1990s. Mathematicians Dolan, Wodak, Hall, and Kaplan (1998) developed a model to estimate HIV incidence in Australian prisons. Data included duration of imprisonment, number of inmates using each needle, lower and higher number of shared injections per IDU per week, proportion of IDUs using bleach, efficacy of bleach, and HIV prevalence and probability of infection. HIV prevalence among IDUs in prison was estimated to have risen 12.2% over 180 weeks.

The United Nations Joint Project on HIV/AIDS reported that as many as one in five inmates are infected with HIV/AIDS in Spanish and Irish jails. The survey of 23 prison systems found the following rates of HIV infection: Denmark (6.6%), Norway (2.9%), Austria (2%), and France (1.9%). The AIDS Conference in Durban addressed HIV in prisons around the world. A recent study of risk factors, especially IDU, among inmates of 22 prisons in seven European nations and found that 13% of IDUs were HIV positive.

The Thai Minister of Public Health reported that 93% of prisoners less than 18 years old at the Bangkok training school for boys were incarcerated for drug-related offenses and they risk HIV infection due to their sexual risk behavior. A 1998 study at 15 Bangkok methadone clinics concluded that between 30-40% of IDUs were infected with HIV (UNAIDS/WHO).

The African National Congress called for the Department of Correctional Services to institute a proper preventative program in prisons, which includes condoms being made available. In addition, the barring of HIV positive individuals from employment in the correctional facilities, and the involuntary segregation of HIV infected inmates were denounced.

The Panafrican News Agency reported that the Office of the Inspecting Judge indicated annual AIDS-related deaths among prisoners in South Africa reached 7,000 in 2006 and would rise to 45,000 in ten years. *Amnesty International* has campaigned against executions in China, the torture of prisoners in Northern Ireland, and the death penalty in the USA. How can effective programs be implemented in Sudan, where civil war has raged for the last 25 years?

Table 2.1 presents data on nations ranked by the rate of incarceration (per 100,000 population) and 2005 estimates of the percentage of the nation's adult (15-49) population with HIV (%HIV). The US has the highest incarceration rate among all nations of the world.

Table 2.1 Ranked Incarceration Rates of Nations with estimates of Percent HIV (2005)

Country	Prisoners/100,000pop.	% HIV(2005est.)
USA	738	0.6
RUSSIAN FED	624	1.1
CUBA	531	0.1
BELIZE	505	2.5
TURKMENISTAN	489	<0.1
BAHAMAS	462	3.3
BELARUS	426	0.3
BARBADOS	367	1.5
PANAMA	364	0.9
SURINAME	356	1.9
SINGAPORE	350	0.3
KAZAKHSTAN	348	0.1
UKRAINE	345	1.4
S.AFRICA	337	18.8
ESTONIA	333	1.3
BOTSWANA	332	24.1
LATVIA	292	0.8
TRINIDAD TOBAGO	288	2.6
KYRGYZSTAN	285	0.1
GEORGIA	276	0.2
MONGOLIA	269	<0.1
NAMIBIA	267	19.6
TUNISIA	263	0.1
GUYANA	260	2.4

Table 2.1 (continued)

Country	Prisoners/100,000pop.	% HIV(2005est.)
CHILE	256	0.3
SWAZILAND	249	33.4
THAILAND	249	1.4
MOLDOVA	247	1.1
POLAND	239	0.1
LITHUANIA	235	0.2
IRAN	214	0.2
BRAZIL	211	0.5
AZERBAIJAN	202	0.1
GABON	196	7.9
MEXICO	196	0.3
URUGUAY	193	0.5
CZECH REP.	186	0.1
COSTA RICA	185	0.3
UZBEKISTAN	184	0.2
N.ZEALAND	183	0.1
RWANDA	183	3.1
JAMAICA	182	1.5
EL SALVADOR	174	0.9
LEBANON	168	0.1
LUXEMBOURG	167	0.2
ARGENTINA	163	0.6
HONDURAS	161	1.5
MOROCCO	161	0.1
SLOVAKIA	158	<0.1

Table 2.1 (continued)

Country	Prisoners/100,000pop.	% HIV(2005est.)
HUNGARY	156	0.1
LESOTHO	156	23.2
ROMANIA	155	<0.1
MAURITIUS	151	0.6
TAJKISTAN	149	0.1
ENGLAND/WALES	149	0.2
BULGARIA	148	<0.1
SPAIN	146	0.6
DOMINICAN REP.	143	1.1
MALAYSIA	141	0.5
BRUNEI DAR.	140	<0.1
SCOTLAND	140	0.2
ZIMBABWE	139	20.1
FIJI	131	0.1
PERU	131	0.6
KENYA	130	6.1
COLOMBIA	129	0.6
NETHERLANDS	128	0.2
ALGERIA	127	0.1
AUSTRALIA	125	0.1
CAMEROON	125	5.4
ZAMBIA	122	17.0
PORTUGAL	121	0.4
MYANMAR	120	1.3
CHINA	118	0.1

Table 2.1 (continued)

Country	Prisoners/100,000pop.	% HIV(2005est.)
SERBIA	117	0.2
NICARAGUA	114	0.2
SRI LANKA	114	<0.1
TANZANIA	113	6.5
MONTENEGRO	108	0.2
PHILIPPINES	108	<0.1
CANADA	107	0.3
BURUNDI	106	3.3
AUSTRIA	105	0.3
VIETNAM	105	0.5
MACEDONIA	99	<0.1
PARAGUAY	97	0.4
S.KOREA	97	<0.1
UGANDA	95	6.7
ECUADOR	94	0.3
GERMANY	93	0.1
BELGIUM	91	0.3
GREECE	90	0.2
MADAGASCAR	90	0.5
ARMENIA	89	0.1
CROATIA	87	<0.1
EGYPT	87	<0.1
MALTA	86	0.1
FRANCE	85	0.4
N.IRELAND	84	0.2

Table 2.1 (continued)

Country	Prisoners/100,000pop.	% HIV(2005est.)
BOLIVIA	82	0.1
SWEDEN	82	0.2
SWITZERLAND	79	0.4
DENMARK	77	0.2
BENIN	75	1.8
FINLAND	75	0.1
REP. BOSNIAHERZ.	74	<0.1
MALAWI	74	14.1
VENEZUELA	74	0.7
REP. IRELAND	72	0.2
LAOS	69	0.1
PAPUA N.GUINEA	69	1.8
ITALY	67	0.5
FED. BOSNIAHERZ.	66	0.1
NORWAY	66	0.1
SLOVENIA	65	<0.1
TOGO	65	3.2
JAPAN	62	<0.1
DJIBOUTI	61	3.1
CAMBODIA	58	1.6
REP. CONGO	57	3.2
GUATEMALA	57	0.9
PAKISTAN	57	0.1
GHANA	55	2.3
BANGLADESH	54	<0.1

Table 2.1 (continued)

Country	Prisoners/100,000pop.	% HIV(2005est.)
SENEGAL	54	0.9
HAITI	52	3.8
INDONESIA	52	0.1
MOZAMBIQUE	51	16.1
COTE D'IVOIRE	49	7.1
NIGER	46	1.1
ANGOLA	44	3.7
ICELAND	40	0.2
REP.GUINEA	37	1.5
SUDAN	36	1.6
CHAD	35	3.5
MALI	33	1.7
GAMBIA	32	2.4
AFGHANISTAN	30	<0.1
COMOROS	30	<0.1
INDIA	30	0.9
NIGERIA	30	3.9
SIERRA LEONE	28	1.6
MAURITANIA	26	0.7
NEPAL	26	0.5
CEN.AFRICA REP.	24	10.7
BURKINA FASO	23	2.0
CONGO	22	5.3

Controlling for the effects of per capita GDP, worldwide rates of HIV/AIDS and incarceration are significantly correlated. These accounts underscore the salience of HIV/AIDS prevention strategies such as fostering knowledge of HIV risk behaviors and viable risk reduction methods. Identifying barriers and facilitators to HIV testing would increase the number of people who are aware of their status. Improving access to effective care and treatment programs can improve the quality of life and survival among persons already infected.

Aggressive follow-up supports are needed to assist released HIV positive inmates in health and treatment related issues. Some progress is being made worldwide. A working meeting was held in Moscow to discuss various strategies. Workshops for "inmate trainers" included, for the first time, 10 female inmates. ITAR-TASS reported that a new prison facility housing only HIV-infected inmates was opened in Irkutsk oblast where medical personnel are specially trained in HIV treatment and prevention. Workshops also convened in Suva. The keynote speaker, Aisea Taoka, the Fiji Commissioner of Prisons, discussed the development of a strategic two-year HIV/AIDS prevention and care program for Fiji's prisons.

The International Harm Reduction Development (IHRD) initiative was formed to reduce HIV infection and drug use in Eastern Europe and the former Soviet Union. A national HIV prevention conference was held in Budapest, and a seminar for prison health personnel was held in Georgia. A pilot project that included the provisions of syringes in Switzerland prisons was successful. Bleach is available to inmates in a growing number of prison systems. The first needle exchange program was initiated in Bilbao Prison, Spain. Drug use did not increase and the program has been expanded to five other prisons. The state government of Sao Paulo began distributing about 100,000 condoms a month in its prisons. The federal government, with support from the World Bank, initiated nine HIV/AIDS prevention projects which also included the distribution of condoms in prisons. The Penitentiary Hospital in Niteroi in Rio de Janeiro is considered a model of good treatment.

The US-funded AIDS Helpline in South Africa is a centralized call center where counselors have access to a continuously updated database of prevention and treatment information. Other projects included home-based care in western Kenya and voluntary HIV testing centers throughout Botswana. The US has promised about $460 million, Britain $41 million, and Canada $22 million to developing nations to battle HIV/AIDS.

Research in the US suggests that between 10-30% of inmates engage in sexual activity, but many prison systems still deny access to condoms. In contrast, condoms are available in Canadian federal penitentiaries and in 23 of the 52 prison systems sampled by the WHO network on HIV/AIDS in prison. No system that has adopted a policy of making condoms available in prisons has reversed that policy. Jamaica's health ministry has no immediate plans to issue condoms to prison inmates but the health and prison ministries were developing an education and training program for inmates and guards. UNAIDS/WHO supports the distribution of condoms and syringes/needles in prisons.

HIV/AIDS AND INCARCERATION IN THE UNITED STATES

About 5% of the world's population lives in the United States. Yet, the US incarcerates about 23% of the world's prisoners (see Hallinan 2001). The CDC estimates that about one million people are living with HIV in the United States. The geographic distribution of HIV infection in the US is uneven but the primary routes of infection among US males were men who have sex with men (MSM), MSM combined with IDU, and IDU. HIV infection among African American women was four times the rate for white women. Research in the US showed that in most cases, upon re-incarceration, the HIV viral load was significantly greater than on first release.

A ranking of the each state by the number of inmates held per 100,000 state population is presented in Table 2.2. National data on the incarceration rate (Rate05 is the number of inmates per 100,000 residents on 30 June 2005) appears in the first column. Louisiana and Georgia incarcerate about 1% of their state population (BJS 2006). The number admitted to incarceration facilities (Admit04) and the number released from incarceration facilities during 2004 (Release04) shows that admissions still outnumber releases. The rate of individuals (AIDS05 is the estimated number of adults and adolescents per 100,000 population) diagnosed with AIDS at the end of 2005 is presented next, followed by the HIV rate (2005) for those states that collect and report the data (CDC 2006).

Table 2.2 Ranked Incarceration Rates of States, numbers of admissions and releases (2004), estimated AIDS and HIV rates (2005)

	IncarRt05	Admit04	Release04	AIDSrt05	HIVrt05
LA	1138	15512	15009	209.7	194.8
GA	1021	20140	18211	218.9	
TX	976	66883	65800	177.3	129.7
MS	955	9187	8607	132.9	176.6
OK	919	9003	8432	67.8	73.1
AL	890	8278	9156	83.4	138.5
FL	835	40386	36908	301.7	225.9
SC	830	9850	10060	182.9	179.2
DE	820	1648	2013	238.2	
AZ	808	11343	10190	98.6	115.5
ID	784	4392	3480	24.3	29.7
NM	782	4279	4090	76.5	54.8
VA	759	11645	11148	128.6	147.3
NV	756	6548	4715	144.4	167.0
TN	732	13149	13295	123.1	126.9
CO	728	8634	8001	102.0	151.1
KY	720	13009	10740	71.1	
MO	715	18281	17307	107.5	98.6
AK	705	2746	2726	60.1	48.7

Table 2.2 (continued)

	IncarRt05	Admit04	Release04	AIDSrt05	HIVrt05
WY	690	769	658	20.3	20.6
CA	682	123537	117762	204.2	
AR	673	8035	7457	87.9	99.3
MI	663	13248	13723	74.5	69.8
WI	653	8071	8596	44.1	48.2
IN	637	16029	15100	74.9	70.5
MD	636	10330	10531	304.6	
SD	622	2304	2428	19.1	28.1
NC	620	10411	9315	117.6	154.8
PA	607	14319	14396	160.6	
KS	582	4519	4683	53.6	52.0
OH	559	28196	28170	74.5	83.3
CT	544	6577	6707	244.6	
NJ	532	13886	14418	245.9	202.9
OR	531	5378	4910	82.6	
MT	526	2182	1897	23.2	
IL	507	39293	38646	153.2	
NY	482	24664	26043	458.7	240.7
UT	466	3275	3050	58.7	42.2
WA	465	11894	11547	98.1	
HI	447	1677	1667	111.8	
WV	443	2267	1946	44.9	41.5
NE	421	2085	2029	47.9	43.3
IA	412	4364	6049	32.6	21.9
ND	359	1008	917	12.7	13.8

Table 2.2 (continued)

	IncarRt05	Admit04	Release04	AIDSrt05	HIVrt05
MA	356	2278	2391	161.6	
NH	319	1099	1080	50.8	
VT	317	2208	2261	41.9	
RI	313	755	828	136.8	
MN	300	6604	5849	50.8	71.5
ME	273	655	636	41.8	
DC				2091.2	
US	738	697066	672202	176.2	136.5
Fed.	62	52982	46624		
State	676	644084	625578		

The strong correlation between the rate of incarceration and HIV/AIDS rates for each state are statistically significant (r= .75 p<.01). About seventeen percent of all persons released from jail and prison are HIV positive (Maddow 2000). Presently, only 18 states test all inmates at admission or while in prison. Correctional facilities lack HIV-specific medical expertise and inmates are typically denied access to basic prevention measures. Comprehensive HIV/AIDS prevention and education programs exist in only 10% of state and federal prisons and 5% of jails. Only two state prison systems (VT and MS) and four jails (New York City, San Francisco, Philadelphia, and Washington, DC) provide condoms to inmates.

Other obstacles to effective HIV detection, treatment, and prevention include language barriers, stigmatization, lack of confidentiality, adherence issues, and a lack of educational skills. Prevention education programs have reduced infection rates inside prisons and jails. In addition, testing and treatment inceptions rise, and treatment outcomes and quality of life improve. Examples of such programs are The Pastoral Case Service and AIDS Education Programs at the California Medical Facility, The COCOA Project in Washington State, and the ACE (AIDS Counseling & Education)

Program at Bedford Hills Correctional Facility in New York. Pilot programs have begun in TX, FL, and within the Federal Bureau of Prisons.

Another innovative project is the Hampden County Correctional Facility in Massachusetts. It has an open door to the community, adopting a health care program based on the public health model that provides inmates with a community-based standard of care (Kahn 2000). When prisoners are released, they continue with the same primary care providers they had inside through a comprehensive discharge plan that includes Medicaid benefits and hookups with other supportive services. Every "pod" at the jail has a regular triage nurse who visits daily.

HIV/AIDS AND INCARCERATION IN DELAWARE

The state of Delaware currently has the 9th highest rate of imprisonment in the nation and it ranks 5th per capita in HIV/AIDS. As compared with other Delaware residents, African American males are more likely to be imprisoned (comprising 19% of the overall state population vs. 63% of the state prison population). According to the Delaware Division of Public Health statistics, the AIDS rate inside its overcrowded prisons is 10 times that of the general population and Delaware prisons have the highest number of AIDS-related deaths in the nation, averaging 18 per year (Bureau of Justice Statistics 2006; Parra and Williams 2005).

At the end of 2004, Delaware reported 3302 AIDS cases to CDC. Prominent in explaining Delaware's high rate of HIV/AIDS infection are its transient populations. Rehoboth Beach is an established gay community that attracts tourists along the east coast of the U.S. In addition, Delaware's thriving poultry industry and neighboring Pennsylvania's mushroom industry employ significant migrant populations. Even more significant for the alarming rate of HIV infection in Delaware, however, is the Interstate-95 and the Amtrak rail system that transits from New York City and Philadelphia in the north, through Delaware's largest city, Wilmington, toward Baltimore and Washington, DC in the south. Unfortunately, these routes are major east coast drug corridors and hence sites of entry for many offenders into Delaware's criminal justice process.

The 2000 census reveals that the state of Delaware has a population of 783,600 of whom 19.2% identify themselves as black. The rate of incarceration per 100,000 Delaware residents for whites is 396 compared to 683 for Hispanics and 2517 for blacks. According to the Delaware Department of Health and Human Services (DHSS 2005) blacks in Delaware are 11 times more likely to die of HIV/AIDS, accounting for 66.2% of the cases, whites account for 28.2%, and Hispanics 5.2%.

According to the Delaware Department of Health and Social Services (2005), those aged 30-39 account for 46% of Delaware's HIV/AIDS cases followed by ages 40-49 (29%), and ages 20-29 (14%). The overall exposure category/transmission modes show that injecting drug use (IDU) accounts for 41.4% of HIV cases in the state, followed by men who have sex with men (MSM) at 30.7%, and 19% result from heterosexual contact.

Delaware's Department of Corrections is the sole government operated correction agency in the state's integrated jail and prison system. It supervises about 5,800 inmates in its facilities and 20,000 probationers in the community, a 30% increase from 1996-1999 (Delaware Statistical Analysis Center 2006). Almost 18,000 offenders are admitted for incarceration yearly. Since the 1980s, the average time served has increased from 25.3 months to 32.7 months (Appendix A). Male inmates account for 235 (8.9%) of the 2,638 total HIV/AIDS cases among males in Delaware and female inmates account for 216 (10.7%) of the 2,016 total cases among females. Unless an inmate is AIDS symptomatic, testing for HIV/AIDS is voluntary.

Therefore, systematic research is required to examine the level of health risk posed by incarceration and community release. Studies have shown that many inmates experience a stressful transition from prison to community (Petersilia 2003; Streetman 2004a; Taxman, Young, and Byrne 2002). Some inmates are now publically discussing the consensual homosexual activity that begins inside prison and then continues outside; released individuals may adopt a bisexual lifestyle, unknown to female partners. Chapter Three outlines the research methodology used in the study of offenders in transition.

3

Research Methodology

Correctional facilities have become prime settings for the development of HIV/AIDS education and prevention programs, and evaluating the kinds of support systems that offenders will need during the transition from prison and reentry into the community (Carney, et al. 1997; Comfort et al. 2000; Grinstead, Zack, and Faigeles 1999b; Kalichman 1998; Mantell et al. 1997; Martin et al. 1993; Martin et al. 1995; Staples 1993; Stevens 1993). To date there has been little systematic study of the health risk behavior among Delaware inmates and on the health risk behavior of newly released inmates.

Testing among 679 Delaware prison inmates eligible for parole or work release from mid-1990 through 1993 found an overall seropostivity rate of 10.2%. The highest rates were among African Americans, Hispanics, persons aged 35 and above, and those with injection drug history (Inciardi, Lockwood, Martin, Pottieger, and Scarpitti 1994). Interviews with inmates at one Delaware prison discovered a "myth of widespread sexual activity," nevertheless, consensual sex was more prevalent than coercive sex (Saum, Surrat, Inciardi, and Bennett 1995).

However, these studies were conducted among male inmates who had been selected to participate in a highly-regimented, therapeutic community (see Inciardi, Martin, Butzin, Hooper, and Harrison 1997; Martin and Inciardi 1997) and, due to their higher motivation, may not be representative of the broader inmate population.

The present research had the long-term objective of understanding the HIV transmission risk posed by incarceration and release back into the community. The project was guided by the following aims: 1) Determine how male inmates within six months of release perceive and experience health-risk behavior; 2) Assess health risk behaviors of newly released inmates; and 3) Identify and adapt an HIV prevention intervention model for inmate pre-release programs.

THEORETICAL APPROACHES

The Age-graded Theory of informal social control maintains that across a person's life, different institutions of both formal and informal social control affect behavior (Sampson and Laub 1993). Social bonds in adulthood, such as marriage and employment, can explain why delinquent activity occurring during adolescence decreases over time. A main focus of much of the research on the transition process from prison is the requirement for offenders to locate legal employment in order to integrate back into society.

HIV risk reduction strategies include several models of intervention that focus on attitudinal changes to precipitate modifications of intentions to engage in risk-reducing actions (Kalichman, 1998). Although the present study was exploratory in design, the data analyses was guided by the following theoretical perspectives. According to the Theory of Reasoned Action (Ajzen and Fishbein 1980; Fishbein and Ajzen 1975), behavior is determined by behavioral intention.

Behavioral intention is defined as the product of an individual's attitude and his/her evaluation of the likely outcomes. The other component of behavioral intention is subjective norm, an individual's perception of what significant others think is important for them, how others might react to a particular behavior, and how motivated the individual is in complying with what others expect from him/her. Utilizing the Reasoned Action Model, the likelihood that an inmate will engage in a particular health risk behavior was assessed with information about the inmate's attitude concerning the behavior and the inmate's perception of how others would react to the behavior.

The Theory of Reasoned Action is similar to Rational Choice Theory (Cohen and Felson 1979; Katz 1980) in that individuals are seen as making conscious and informed decisions about whether to engage in particular behaviors. Competing perspectives posit that decision making is impeded because rational choices are bounded by the complexity of situations and by the availability of resources (Bachrach & Baratz 1962; Simon 1957).

Additional theoretical approaches were used in order to identify and adapt possible intervention models. The Social Cognitive Model approaches learning as a social process influenced by interactions with other people (Bandura 1977). The basic components are the physical and social environments that shape and reinforce the beliefs determining behavior, and a person's belief that he/she is capable of performing the new behavior in the new situation (self-efficacy). Accepting that harmful behaviors exist, the primary goal of the Harm Reduction model is to offer ways to reduce the negative consequences of the targeted behavior (Brettle 1991).

The Aids Risk Reduction Model maintains that in order to change behavior, the behavior must first be seen as risky, this is followed by a commitment to change the behavior, and then action taken to perform the desired change (Catania, Kegeles, and Coates 1990). Importantly, social norms, fear, and anxiety may influence the movements between stages. The Health Belief Model focuses on the key elements of decision making such as an individual's perception of susceptibility, the perceived severity of the risk, and the perceived barriers to protection (Rosenstock, Strecher, and Becker 1994).

Finally, five steps are outlined in the Stages of Change Intervention: precontemplation, contemplation, preparation, action, and maintenance (Prochaska, DiClemente, and Norcross 1992). Each of these models highlights essential components of intervention approaches that were adapted to the specific health risk needs of post release inmates.

HYPOTHESES

Based on the theoretical and empirical literature the following relationships are hypothesized.

Table 3.1 Research Hypotheses

An offender would be MORE likely to engage in HIV risk behaviors during the release and reentry transition if he/she:

H1: had more extensive alcohol/drug histories;

H2: had no or few supportive relationships;

H3: measured lower on knowledge about HIV/AIDS risk prevention;

H4: measured lower on behavioral intention to avoid specific HIV/AIDS risks;

H5: perceived greater barriers to specific HIV/AIDS risk avoidance.

H6: These variables would exert a cumulative effect on the magnitude of HIV risk behaviors occurring during the release/reentry transition.

MEASURES

The data collection instruments appear in Appendix C. Each data collection inventory was constructed with the assistance of an inmate representative and pretested on a sample of offenders to adjust for reading and comprehension level. In addition to collecting demographic information such as age and level of education, an Alcohol/Drug Severity Index asked subjects about 10 types of illegal drugs and/or non-medical use of prescription drugs, including the age of first use, the frequency of use, and periods of heavy use. Offenders were asked about the number and types of relationships and friendships to assess their level of social support. Knowledge about HIV/AIDS and the risks associated with HIV/AIDS was measured by a 25-item true/false questionnaire. HIV/AIDS risk history was measured by an 11-item "Have you ever … (check all that apply)" inventory.

Scores for the *subjective norm* and *motivation to comply* components of Behavioral Intention were calculated using a 24-item questionnaire that asked subjects to mark along a 0 to 10 continuum where "very unlikely" was at one end and "very likely" at the other end to a series of specific HIV risk or risk avoidance behaviors. Consistent with the Theory of Reasoned Action, these scores were multiplied for the Behavioral Intention Score. A similar continuum ("very easy" on one end to "very hard" at the other end) was used to assess the level of perceived barriers to specific health protection and risk avoidance activities.

Collecting both quantitative and qualitative data was desirable because little is known about this population and the results will be used to create structured measures, generate hypotheses, and design culturally sensitive questionnaires and risk prevention programs in subsequent research. Knowledge of the participants' culture, the ability to recruit and develop rapport, to listen well, to probe without creating negative interaction, and record responses in an unobtrusive manner proved essential to successful interviewing of offenders.

The present research adapted two data collection instruments to the research sites: the Goal Attainment/Functional Status Assessment (Rapkin, Smith, Dumont, Correa, Palmer, and Cohen 1994) and the Information, Motivation, and Behavioral Skills (IMB) Interview (Misovich, Fisher, and Fisher 1998). The IMB model of AIDS risk behavior change has been developed and validated to serve as a general conceptualization for understanding and promoting AIDS risk reduction behavior change.

The questionnaire took approximately 45 minutes to complete when used in a university student population and included the following sections: Demographic Measures, AIDS Prevention Information Measures, Measures of Motivation to Perform AIDS Preventive Behavior, Attitudes toward AIDS preventive acts, Subjective norms regarding AIDS preventive acts, Behavioral intentions for AIDS prevention, Behavioral skills measures, and AIDS Preventive Behaviors. Following the interviews, data were coded and analyzed utilizing the Statistical Package for Social Sciences software (SPSS).

SAMPLE & STUDY SITES

The sample consisted of incarcerated men in Delaware's Department of Correction who were participating in Pre-release Programs (signifying that they were within six months of release). All of the inmates in the facilities were over 18 years of age. Following meetings with the Treatment Administration staff, fifty (50) English-speaking individuals, able to give consent, were targeted to ensure that volunteers who were recruited represented variations in known risk characteristics: over 30 years old, incarcerated at least 2 years, and had a history of HIV-risk behavior.

The rationale for the selection criteria follows. This research was designed to devise culturally-sensitive data collection instruments and collect exploratory data. While data could be collected on all inmates who meet the aforementioned criteria, African American subjects were targeted for participation due to the high rates of HIV transmission risk among this group. Furthermore, the inclusion of other groups would confound the design of the data collection instruments and present additional challenges in the analysis of data. The devastating effects of the AIDS epidemic on the African American community necessitated a focused approach. The inclusion and exclusion criteria were:

Inclusion Criteria:

* English-speaking inmates
* inmates over 29 years of age
* inmates who had been incarcerated at least 2 years
* inmates who were able and gave consent to participate
* inmates who were enrolled in the Pre-release program
* inmates who identified themselves as black or African-American
* inmates who reported/demonstrated a history of any of health-risk behavior(s):
  - tatooing prior to or during incarceration
  - drug use prior to or during incarceration
  - unprotected sexual activity prior to or during incarceration;

Exclusion Criteria:

* * individuals under 30 years of age
* * those incarcerated less than 2 years
* * those who reported no history of health risk behavior(s)
* * individuals who did not speak and understand English
* * inmates who did not identify themselves as black or African-American.

Inmates in the Pre-release Programs at DCC in Smyrna, DE and at the Multi-Purpose Criminal Justice Facility in Wilmington, DE were successfully recruited to participate in the present study. At any given time these research sites house over 60 inmates who are eligible for release from prison within six months. Official permission was obtained to conduct interviews with inmates at these sites.

A systematic selection process ensured that only volunteers were recruited. Participants were recruited individually, had the consent form read to them, and were given the opportunity to ask questions, free from group pressure. As an incentive and as compensation for their participation, inmates had $10.00 credited toward their institutional account. Consent for post-release contact was also obtained at this time. Post-release interviewees would receive a $50.00 money order for their participation. Those recruited were English-speaking, at least 18 years of age, and able to give consent to participate. Due to budgetary considerations, non-English-speaking inmates, and adolescents were excluded, however, subsequent funding will be sought to address these populations.

Meetings took place with staff, counselors, and inmate representatives at the Multi-Purpose Criminal Justice Facility in Wilmington, Delaware. The counselors and inmate representatives felt that the age selection criteria was too narrow (those aged 30 would detect intravenous drug users but sexual risk behavior usually begins at earlier ages). Therefore, the age inclusion criteria was lowered to 24. The semi-structured interview instrument was approved for use by each facility. Following meetings with the Treatment Administrator and Treatment Counselors, announcements were posted and read to all Pre-release Program participants describing the project and asking for volunteers. A Treatment Counselor served as a contact person, and with the Principal Investigator, made a presentation in the Pre-release Program classrooms to those interested in volunteering for the study. The presentation introduced the Principal Investigator, provided background information on health risks, and described the research design. A question and answer session followed. Potential participants were screened to ensure that they met the selection criteria, and each person was given the opportunity to ask questions.

The Delaware State University Institutional Review Board, Human Subjects Committee approved the project, however modifications to the research design required that the application be reconsidered. Therefore, the revised application was re-approved by the DSU IRB. The Delaware Bureau of Prisons also has a review board which approved of the project before any inmates were contacted. In accordance with the OPRR Reports *Protection of Human Subjects, Title 45, Code of Federal Regulations, Part 46, Subpart C-Additional DHHS Protections Pertaining to Biomedical and Behavioral Research Involving Prisoners as Subjects*, at least one member of the IRB must be a prisoner or prisoner representative. In this case a representative from the Delaware Council on Justice (formerly the Prisoners' Aid Society) served on the review board (see Appendix B).

As the Principal Investigator, I was required to pass a background investigation that permitted me to conduct research in the prisons. In meetings with the Delaware Department of Corrections Administration I was made aware that if an inmate had plans to harm himself or someone else, or abuse a child, that this information must be reported to the authorities. This research project posed no physical, physiological, or legal risks to participants. Some questions concerning the subjects' health and health risks were personal in nature, and due to the potential stigmatizing nature of deviant behavior, the data collected was protected from unauthorized persons. The information obtained was analyzed and reported at the group level.

Having established rapport with the Treatment Administrator, the DOC counseling staff, and inmate group leaders reduced the likelihood of participant risk. These personnel assisted in identifying those subjects who best met the selection criteria, including previous HIV-risk behavior. Moreover, they used their expertise, both in the institutional climate and with the factors that may have contributed to incarceration, when helping to adapt the data collection instruments to the specific research site and in protecting participants from potential risks.

The input provided by Treatment staff and inmate Pre-release Program group leaders resulted in direct benefits to the prison population by raising the level of health risk awareness among inmates and correctional staff. Inmate morale also benefitted from the knowledge that they were responsible for making valuable contributions to scientific research and improving the health of inmates and the broader community. Each individual was made aware of the valuable scientific and social contribution that they were making by their participation, thereby outweighing any potential risk of revealing stigmatizing information.

Finally, the knowledge gained from this project provided vital information enabling the design and implementation of custom intervention models to protect inmate communities from health risks. The devastating effects of the AIDS epidemic on the African American community necessitates innovative approaches. Little is known about the HIV transmission risk posed by incarceration and release in the community. Given the precautions and measures taken to ensure confidentiality of participants, the anticipated benefits to subjects, their families, and communities outweigh potential risks. The risks must be considered reasonable in relation to the importance of the research findings that resulted from this project. The next chapter provides an overview of the interviews with inmates during pre-release.

4

Anticipating Release

The data for this study was collected from 73 in-depth interviews. Forty-five inmates in pre-release programs at two incarceration facilities in Delaware were interviewed during 2001–2002. These sites typically house over 60 inmates who are eligible for release from prison within six months.[1] Subjects were over-sampled, anticipating unsuccessful attempts to re-contact and re-interview this baseline sample of pre-release inmates.

Pre-release interviews were conducted on a voluntary basis in a private setting. Treatment staff were on hand to provide assistance to individuals who indicated a desire or need for additional counseling. As stated in the informed consent form, participation or nonparticipation did not result in any penalty. A participant could also decide to discontinue participation at any time without penalty. No names appeared on interview or other data collection forms, only a code number was used for identification purposes. The informed consent forms were kept in a locked metal file cabinet located at Delaware State University where access was limited; it was not shared with any DOC staff members or other persons in DOC facilities. The location of the interview rooms provided a secure and confidential setting for non-threatening interaction and protected the subject from possible risks. Given the elaborate

---

1. The only pre-release females interviewed were those at the work-release center; interviews at the female incarceration facility were not granted. Therefore some data is not available for subsequent pre-/post-release comparative analyses.

procedures and precautions taken to ensure confidentiality, the potential risks were minimized.

At each facility I was greeted at the main gate by a senior counselor/liaison and escorted to an interview room. The rooms at one facility were part of a new prison addition. The warden at this site approved the recording of interviews, with inmates' consent. At the other facility, I was escorted to a residential pod, where I interviewed inmates in a small office. No recording was permitted there.

The Informed Consent Form was read to each participant. The volunteer must have understood and signed the informed consent form to participate in the proposed research. Volunteers could examine the form and have a copy. During the first interview subjects were asked for a contact address where a second interview could take place. Since most inmates experience a high degree of uncertainty during the transition period following release, the Delaware Bureau of Community Corrections provided assistance in re-contacting offenders following their release from prison. I attempted to interview offenders within two months of release. Despite having the subject's contact phone number and address, and an offer of a $50.00 money order as an added incentive, making contact was more challenging and time-consuming than anticipated.[2] The elapsed time from release to interview averaged six months.

In agreement with the Delaware Bureau of Prisons, I had limited access to participants' background information for verification purposes. All data that was collected during interviews with the respondents was used for research purposes only. No attempt was made to stratify the sample by HIV status due to the voluntary nature of HIV testing in Delaware's DOC. As seen in Table 4.1, forty-five inmates were interviewed during 2001–2002.

---

2. Eleven released offenders did not respond to repeated efforts to contact them; the telephone/address contact information proved invalid for 7; 6 inmates were never released or were re-incarcerated soon after being released; 3 died before I could re-contact them (see Binswanger, Stern, Deyo, Heagerty, Cheadle, Elmore, and Koepsell 2007; Parra and Williams 2005); one changed his mind about being re-interviewed.

Table 4.1: Interview time frame by location and gender

Year 2001–2002 (N=45)

Incarceration Facility A:	24 male inmates
Incarceration Facility B:	21 male inmates
Total:	45 male inmates

Years 2002–2006 (N=28)

Work-release Center:	4 males; 6 females
In the community:	13 males; 5 females
Total:	17 males; 11 females

Twenty-eight interviews with released male and female offenders were conducted during 2002-2006. Seventeen males had been previously interviewed while incarcerated. Four of the male interviews and six of the female interviews were conducted at a work-release center.

Forty-four of the male inmates identified themselves as African American or black, one identified himself as black/Hispanic. Nine of the females identified themselves as African American or black and two identified themselves as "mixed/white." Six females were interviewed at the work-release facility, the remaining five had been released from DOC custody. The ages of the females ranged from 19 to 45 years old. Their length of incarceration ranged from four months to seven years. Of the four released females, the elapsed time since release ranged from 85 days to over one year.

As seen in Table 4.2, male offenders, on average, were older and had been incarcerated longer than female offenders. Females averaged slightly more years of education and more females reported that they were single/not in a relationship. All offenders reported past alcohol/drug abuse with females reporting fewer drug-free friends. Female offenders reported more HIV risk behaviors while the males scored slightly higher on the HIV/AIDS knowledge test (average number correct out of 25 questions).

Table 4.2: Descriptive analyses of Offenders by gender

	Males (N=45)	Females (N=11)	Total (N=56)
age	37.8	32.3	36.7
years education	10.8	11.0	10.8
months incarcerated	65.2	28.4	58.1
% single/not in relationship	50%	55%	51%
% past alcohol/drug abuse	100%	100%	100%
friends w/o drug problem	2.4	0.9	2.1
HIV risk behaviors	4.0	5.1	4.2
HIV/AIDS knowledge score	21.9	21.5	21.8

HIV RISK BEHAVIORS PRIOR TO AND DURING INCARCERATION

All of the male offenders had at least one risk behavior and 16 had at least five risk behaviors. All of the females reported at least two risk behaviors and half had at least five risk behaviors. As seen in Table 4.3, the most frequent risk behavior was having sex without using a latex condom, followed by having unprotected sex while under the influence of alcohol/drugs. Almost two-thirds of both males and females reported having unprotected sex with more than one partner at a time. Sixty-four percent of the females had been infected with, or had sex with someone infected with, a sexually-transmitted disease as compared to 56% of the males.

Table 4.3: Percent engaging in HIV Risks prior to and during Incarceration by gender

	Males (N=45)	Females (N=11)
had sex with man or woman without using latex condom	89%	100%
mixed unprotected sex with alcohol or other drugs	76	82
had unprotected sex with more than one partner at a time	64	64
been infected by or had sex with someone infected with STD	56	64
received or given sex for drugs and/or money	33	64
had sex with someone who used injection drugs	29	45
had same-sex sex without using latex condom	20	45
injection drug use	29	27
shared a needle or syringe with another person to inject drugs	11	27
been tatooed with unsterilized needles	11	27
Average HIV/AIDS risk history score=	4.0	5.1

Almost two-thirds of the females had received or given sex for drugs and/or money as compared to one-third of the males. Forty-five percent of the females had sex with someone who used injection drugs as compared to 29% of the males. Forty-five percent of the females also reported having same-sex sex without using a latex condom as compared to 20% of the males. More males reported injecting drugs. But a higher percentage of females reported sharing needles to inject drugs and being tatooed with an unsterilized needle.

In sum, female offenders measured significantly higher on past HIV/AIDS risks.

CONCERNS DURING PRISON RELEASE

Table 4.4 shows the top-ranked concerns reported by males and females during pre-release. "How to make amends to my family", "finding a place to live", and "finding a job/how to get money" were the top-ranked concerns facing males during the pre-release period. "Change myself", "deal with my sentence", and "kids" were the top-ranked concerns for females.

Table 4.4: Top-ranked Concerns during Pre-release by gender

Males (N=45):	Females (N=11):
how to make amends to family	change myself
finding a place to live	deal with my sentence (years)
finding a job/how to get money	kids
anxiety over release/re-offending	relationship with another inmate
finding a new girlfriend	"bugging out" or "snapping"
coming out with nothing	requesting medical care
safety/don't want to die in prison	religious beliefs

Overall, there is remarkably little similarity between the males' and females' concerns during pre-release. A close examination of the concerns reveals that there is much anxiety surrounding the transition from prison and the work-release facility. Chapter Five examines how the released offenders adjusted to the transition back to family and work roles in the community.

5

Good to be Out, What Next?

Every offender offered a distinctive biography. For example, "Ruth" was referred to me by another released offender. She was about 35 years old and had been in and out of prison for several years. She ran away from home when she was 14 years old because her stepfather had been sexually abusing her since she was 7 (her brother began abusing her a few years later). Within twenty minutes of her arrival at the bus terminal in New York she was approached by a man who took her in. He provided her with a place to stay, clothes, drugs, and love. One night he told her to put on a wig to help him make some money. Thus began her life as a prostitute. She eventually began injecting drugs. One day during an argument, she shot and killed her pimp. Ruth was convicted and transferred to prison.

In prison Ruth had many lovers. One guard would let her slip into her partner's cell to make love. Other times she would skip breakfast to spend time with her lover when the cell doors were unlocked. Women would make love in the showers too. Everyone knew about HIV but no one seemed to care much about protecting themselves from it. Just before Ruth was released she heard that her mother had died from AIDS. Ruth decided to get tested. She reported that after living most of her life doing drugs and selling sex, she had tested negative. Now she wants to protect herself from infection. The only drug she does is cigarettes.

In another case, a young man I must call "?" claimed that he was released without any documentation. He could not get a job that required a driver's license because he did not have a birth certificate or a Social

Security card. Fortunately for him, his long-time girlfriend was providing a place for him to stay.

The post-release interviews were conducted in a variety of locations across the state. Interview subjects were eager to discuss their situation and each expressed a willingness to be interviewed again if needed. All subjects were on probation, although at different levels of supervision. Four of the interviews were conducted at a work-release center. This highly-regimented environment gradually permitted offenders release time for job-interviews, work, and eventually to be "signed-out" by a sponsor overnight and on weekend furloughs.

TRANSITION FROM PRISON

The transition from prison necessitates re-establishing family and work roles in the community (Streetman 2004b). The difficulties that released offenders encountered were inversely related to the availability of a support network. The average age of interview subjects (37 years) is regarded as a period of the most productive years of the lifecourse. However, the most recent 8-9% of these individuals' lives have been characterized by extreme stress and isolation. The need for emotional support and intimacy was evident in all of the interviews and this was reflected in the release priorities.

Subjects described their first day out as one spent with family, enjoying a meal together, followed by talking and relaxing around the television. Extended family members were present or dropped by at some point. Two subjects reported spending the entire day in bed with their girlfriend. Most of the interview subjects reported avoiding contact with old friends.

Table 5.1 displays the transition characteristics of the released male and female offenders. Seventy-one percent of the released males had stable housing and 59% had access to medical care. This compared to 82% of the females with stable housing and access to medical care. However, this included four males and six females who were still required to stay at the work release center. About one-quarter of the released males were still seeking employment as compared to 73% of the released females. Seven of the females were seeking employment at the time of interview.

Table 5.1: Transition characteristics of Released Offenders by gender

	Males (N=17)	Females (N=11)
stable housing (included work-release)	71%	82%
access to medical care (included work-release)	59	82
seeking employment	24	73
in relationship(s)	59	55
had HIV test since release	35	91

In the initial interviews only one inmate identified himself as "married"; fourteen males identified themselves as "single"; two reported being "coupled to a female partner". By the time of the second interview, however, several relationships had changed. Fifty-nine percent of the released male offenders were in a female partner relationship. Seven released males had formed relationships with female partners and one previously coupled male was single.

Four male offenders met their female partner while assigned to the work-release center. Over half (55%) of the released females reported that they were in a relationship (five were coupled to a male partner, and one female reported that she was coupled to both a male partner and a female partner). Two subjects met their female partner while assigned to a work-release center (each reported having sex in a closet at the center).

Only 35% of the released male offenders had been tested for HIV since being released (an additional subject stated that he was tested the night before he was released from prison). All but one female had been tested for HIV since being released from the women's correctional center. Three females reported that they were HIV positive and were taking medications as prescribed.

REESTABLISHING FAMILY AND WORK ROLES

When asked about present living arrangements, five males told me that they lived with a parent (one stayed with his father whose apartment was directly over a tavern); four lived with girlfriends; one lived with his sister's family; one subject was staying in a motel. All four subjects at the work-release center planned to live with their mother or girlfriend.

Twelve subjects reported having one or more children. When asked about their goals, four subjects responded "getting married." Other responses also showed the importance of re-establishing family relationships: "spend time with my family"; "be a better parent"; "get back with my children's mom and be a family again"; "have my son come stay with me"; "buy a house and have all of my children stay with me"; "reconnect with my children and make up for lost time, be a part of their life"; "be a father again".

Six subjects reported no present job (included is one who could not work and received disability from an accident, and one waiting for space in a treatment half-way house). Three were employed in construction, two worked in restaurants, two worked in transportation/delivery, and one worked as a night janitor. Several of the subjects mentioned seeking an additional job, or a better-paying job, in order to pay off fines and begin saving money for a house. Having a house was seen as instrumental in re-establishing a family and the role of father.

DIFFICULTIES ENCOUNTERED
DURING RELEASE TRANSITION

Responses to "What has been the *most* difficult part of your transition back outside?" included: "feel like I am under a microscope"; "no relationships, no sex"; "getting the type of job I want"; "looking for a job takes more effort, in prison the jobs are right there for you"; "with the weather changing, it will be tougher to work outdoors"; "don't have freedom to come and go"; "getting re-established, couldn't prove my identity".

Other responses included "everything was different, people on the street got meaner"; "making enough money to save"; "not being able to see my sons"; "seeing my grandfather in his condition"; "dealing with a nervous feeling, still feel like something is hanging over me"; "adjusting and putting everything behind me".

Responses to "What parts of the transition were *easier* than you expected?" included: "got a job right away"; "getting a job"; "getting rides to job interviews"; "getting rides, people helping me get clothes"; "getting a roof over my head"; "making phone calls with phone cards"; "strong support group"; "everyone was happy to see me"; "I can talk about my feelings with someone"; "interacting with society, I expected everything to be speeded up"; "being able to accept my situation, being on my own for the first time"; "adapting, I don't feel paranoid about how people are going to look at me". Three subjects reported "none" or "nothing."

PRIORITIES, GOALS, AND HEALTH CONCERNS

As seen in Table 5.2, males ranked "get own place", "get married", and "find employment" at the top of their concerns during post-release, while female offenders ranked "get GED", "find job/job training", and "get family back living together" at the top of their concerns. Comparing pre-release concerns with concerns during reentry reveals that priorities among males (finding a place to live, employment, reestablishing relationships, and anxiety about completing probation) remained relatively similar. Among females, the priorities during incarceration were distinct from those during release/reentry transition. Only "kids" and "getting family back together" were similar priorities.

Table 5.2: Top-ranked Concerns in Post-release by gender

Males (N=17):	Females (N=11):
get own place	get GED/complete education
get married	find job/job training
find employment	get family back living together
complete probation	get house/home
reestablish family	maintain sponsor/relationships

Other responses to "What are your top concerns and priorities right now?" from the released females included "none"; "want to see my mom, but I need permission"; "staying with my recovery"; "not enough shelters for men and women". Females responded to "What are some things you'd like to accomplish?" with items related to education, employment, family and home, and health/treatment. Specific responses about education included: "get GED"; "get cosmetology career started"; "go to school and stay in"; "go to college for fashion design"; "go to school and get beauticians license"; "go to college"; "finish high school". Specific responses about jobs and employment included: "get a nice job"; "own restaurant"; "open youth center"; "teach work of God"; "get job with good medical and dental benefits"; "find a job"; "be an accountant".

Female responses about family and home included: "help take care of mom" ;"get married"; "have three kids"; "being a spouse"; "have a family"; "get house and sons back with me"; "make sure sons don't drink, do drugs or go to jail"; "get my son with my husband"; "get a nice house"; "get my own apartment"; "move out of apartment into a house"; "get my own place"; "see sons go off and get married"; "get daughter back living with me"; "want children to finish school"; "own house"; "have a big house and yard for my children"; "want to buy land for a house". Other responses included: "taking care of responsibilities"; "having fun"; "get a nice car".

When males were asked "Have you sought health care?" four responded "No." Two males reported that health benefits are provided through their employer. One reported that he has medical benefits as part of his mother's coverage. Five males have sought health care since their release for the following conditions: asthma, chest pain/high cholesterol, seizures, diabetes, and stomach pains. Four reported that they wished to get a complete physical examination.

Other concerns among the released males included: "concerned about hepatitis C because of past IV drug use"; "want to lose weight and stop smoking"; "kidney pain"; "throbbing headaches"; and "concerned about anthrax". Several responded that they do not have time for recreation but that their job requires physical activity.

When asked "Do you have any health concerns, or have you sought health care?", all of the females reported that they had sought health care. One female reported that she has been taking medication for asthma. Another reported that she is taking medication for high blood pressure. One female reported that she suffers from anxiety, depression and mood swings. Other responses included: "had a check up"; "have chest pain"; "problem with leg, knee, and back, had surgery on my knee"; "had a operation"; "went to family doctor to check for diabetes".

When asked "Is protecting your health a major concern for you?" eight females responded "Yes" and two responded "No". Additional comments included "hard to get health insurance"; "even with Medicaid it's hard to get dental care"; "I try to have healthy habits". Specific responses about health/treatment included: "Get life back on track"; "working and keeping a sponsor"; "maintain sobriety".

Table 5.3 compares the average number of times that male and female offenders had engaged in various activities since being released from prison. Offenders had gone to religious services about five times since their release, with females attending more than males. Discussing safe sex with partner(s) and buying or receiving latex condoms averaged over four times, with females doing this more times than males. Released male offenders had gone on a "date" more times than females. Females were significantly more likely to have gone on job interviews as compared to males (this may be because the majority of males found employment soon after release).

Females had also sought out information concerning safe sex, on average, over five times as compared to less than three for males.

Table 5.3: Average times in various activities during reentry by gender

	Males (N=17)	Females (N=11)	Total
gone to religious services	4.2	5.8	4.8
discussed safe sex with partner	3.7	6.1	4.6
bought or received latex condoms	3.9	5.7	4.6
gone on a "date"	4.6	3.4	4.1
gone on a job interview	1.9	6.4	3.7***
sought out information concerning safe sex	2.5	5.4	3.6
encouraged someone to get tested for HIV	1.8	5.3	3.1**
had sex while under influence alcohol/drugs	1.8	2.5	2.1
gone out looking for any kind of excitement	0.8	3.5	1.8*
had sex with someone hardly knew	1.4	1.6	1.5

*p<.1   **p<.05   ***p<.01

All but two males said that they had been on "dates" following their release from prison; four had been on more than ten dates. Four males reported that they had sex with a stranger following their release from prison, three had done this more than once. Six males reported that they had sex while under the influence of alcohol since their release, four had done this more than once. One male reported that he had unprotected sex three times since being released.

Four males had been tested for HIV since being released (an additional subject stated that he was tested the night before he was released from prison). Five reported that they had sought out information on HIV/AIDS. Seven males reported that they had encouraged someone to get tested for HIV. Eleven said that they had discussed safe sex with their partner(s) at least once. Twelve stated that they had bought or received condoms at least once (condoms are readily available at the work-release center, unlike in prison).

Six of the female subjects indicated that they had been sexually active since their release from the women's correctional center. Three of these six reported multiple sex partners and each reported that they had engaged in unprotected sex at least once. Three females also reported having sex while at the work-release center. Three females indicated that they had sex while under the influence of alcohol/drugs and one female reported having sex for drugs since her release. Nine females reported that they had encouraged someone to get tested for HIV. Eight females said that they had discussed safe sex with their partner(s) at least once. Eight females stated that they had bought or received condoms at least once. Seven females reported that they had sought out information concerning safe sex.

Females were significantly more likely to encourage someone to get tested for HIV (over five times) as compared to males. On average, offenders had sex while under the influence of alcohol/drugs twice. Females were significantly more likely to go out looking for any kind of excitement (3.5 times) as compared to the males (less than once). Both males and females had had sex with someone they hardly knew at least once.

In summary, females reported more sexual activity than did the released male offenders. A lack of financial support may have placed two female offenders at a heightened risk of engaging in sex work. One female reported going back to selling drugs as the only way to make ends meet. Another female reported that the father of her son was a drug dealer and she had no other means of support.

The interviews revealed that male offenders encountered less difficulty in obtaining employment. This probably is due to the availability of construction and manual labor jobs that typically employ males. Several males mentioned seeking an additional job, or a better-paying job, in order to pay off fines and begin saving money for a house. Having a house was seen as instrumental in re-establishing a family and re-assuming the role of provider. The majority of the released male offenders had stable housing and access to medical care.

Few males mentioned education, yet all of the female offenders mentioned education as one way to improve their life chances. Most of the released male offenders had jobs, stable housing, and access to medical care. While many were involved in stable relationships, the transition period still involved sexual risk-taking, particularly multiple partners. The majority maintained that they always used condoms. But only two mentioned abstinence as a way to protect their health. Overall, the release priorities reflected the degree to which offenders received various types of support from family and/or intimate partners. But HIV/AIDS prevention was viewed as a separate concern, distinct from other priorities (Streetman 2006).

Why did many of the released offenders engage in risky behaviors despite previous intentions to avoid them? This is the topic of the next chapter.

6

When Good Intentions Go Bad

Criminologists claim that the single best predictor of criminal behavior is past criminal behavior. Unfortunately, predicting any human behavior is problematic, particularly when individuals face uncertainty. This chapter will explore the relationship between the measures of behavioral intention of the inmates who were interviewed prior to release, with their actual behaviors during the transition from incarceration. As outlined in Chapter Three, the Theory of Reasoned Action is a model of decision-making which maintains that behavioral intention is the best predictor of individual behavior.

Empirical research demonstrates that much of human behavior is habitual and many decisions involve inductive reasoning because choices are limited by the availability of information and the complexity of situations (Arp III 2004; Arthur 1994; Boyd and Richerson 2002; Frisch and Baron 1988; Pfeffer 1981; Russo and Schoemaker 1989; Shover and Honaker 1996; Stincombe 1990). Some interesting research has shown that children tend to make more risky choices than adults (Levin, Hart, Weller, and Harshman, in press), peers exert a stronger impact on risky decision making among adolescents than adults, and that risky decision making decreases with age (Gardner and Steinberg 2005; Streetman 1996).

Situational context is an important component of risky decision making. In jails and prison the consequences of risk behaviors may appear remote (Schmid and Jones 1996; Streetman 2006). The decision making process is affected by emotions and by levels of arousal (Peters, Vastfjall,

Garling, and Slovic 2006). Research has demonstrated that individuals adopt safer sexual behaviors if they can be taught to focus on the feelings of regret that they will experience later for having engaged in unsafe sex practices (Richard, Van de Plight, and De Vries 1998).

The target object also affects decision making. In relationships, some individuals are more likely to make risky decisions for others than for themselves (Wray and Stone 2005). Weber, Blais, and Betz (2002) developed a risk-attitude scale showing five distinct decision domains: financial, health/safety, recreational, ethical, and social. According to their research, males are less risk-averse in all domains except social.

Many offenders have documented histories of alcohol/drug abuse that distorts decision making so that relapse is a constant challenge among released offenders. According to DeJong, Finn, Grand, and Markoff (1994), relapse predictors include a background of severe addiction, a weak employment history, and a criminal record. Learning to recognize and disrupt the seemingly innocuous series of "decision chains" that expose offenders to the risks of relapse is compounded by the nature and level of difficulties encountered during the release and reentry transition period.

Table 6.1 shows the impact of length of incarceration (those who have been incarcerated 3 years or less compared to those who have been incarcerated longer than three years) on several variables of interest. As might be expected, those incarcerated longer are older. But they are also less educated, and slightly more likely to be single/not in a relationship. They measured lower on knowledge about HIV/AIDS, and were less likely to have been tested for HIV in the last six months. They also averaged a lower number of HIV risk behaviors. Regardless of length of incarceration, the vast majority of those interviewed had a history of alcohol and drug abuse.

Table 6.1: Characteristics of Male Inmates by Length of Incarceration

	3 years or less (N=27)	longer than 3 yrs. (N=18)	Total (N=45)
Average age	33.0	44.9	37.7
Average years education	11.3	10.6	11.0
Single/not in relationship	63%	67%	64%
% correct on HIV knowledge quiz	92%	84%	88%
% tested for HIV w/i last 6 mo.	70%	22%	51%
Average number of risk behaviors	4.0	3.8	3.9
% past alcohol/drug abuse	100%	94%	98%

A detailed alcohol/drug history was taken of all 45 of the incarcerated males (Table 6.2). All but one inmate reported heavy alcohol use prior to incarceration. The median age at which alcohol use began was 14. Almost ninety percent reported heavy marijuana use prior to incarceration. Over sixty percent reported cocaine use prior to incarceration and over twelve percent reported injecting drug use prior to incarceration. As can be seen from the average age at onset, drug use typically proceeded from alcohol and marijuana during adolescence, to pills and harder drugs during young adulthood.

Table 6.2: Alcohol/drug history among male inmates (N=45)

	Average age at first use	% ever using
alcohol	14.0	100.0
marijuana	14.4	87.5
pills "uppers"	19.6	41.7
pills "downers"	20.4	37.5
heroin	21.5	41.7
hallucinogens	21.6	29.2
cocaine (non-IV)	22.7	62.5
IV drug use	23.0	12.5
crack/freebase	24.5	54.2

alcohol/drug history average score = 30.0

As discussed in Chapter Three, in addition to demographic information, and the Alcohol/Drug Severity Index, offenders were asked about the number and types of relationships and friendships to assess their level of social support. Knowledge about HIV/AIDS and the risks associated with HIV/AIDS was measured by a 25-item true/false questionnaire. HIV/AIDS risk history was measured by an 11-item "Have you ever … (check all that apply)" inventory.

Also, scores for the *subjective norm* and *motivation to comply* components of Behavioral Intention were calculated using a 24-item questionnaire that asked subjects to mark along a 0 to 10 continuum where "very unlikely" was at one end and "very likely" at the other end to a series of specific HIV risk or risk avoidance behaviors. Consistent with the Theory of Reasoned Action, these scores were multiplied for the Behavioral Intention Score. A similar continuum ("very easy" on one end to "very hard" at the other end) was used to assess the level of perceived barriers to specific health protection and risk avoidance activities.

Table 6.3 displays the ranked behavioral intention scores of the 17 inmates who were re-interviewed after reentering the community. Getting their partner(s) tested received the highest score followed by using latex condoms. Intending to have latex condoms handy, getting tested for HIV, and having partner(s) practice safer sex were also seen as likely. Intending to buy latex condoms, discussing safer sex were less likely, and the likelihood of not having sex during the transition and reentry period appeared remote.

The effects of significant others' influence on offenders' intentions and the offender's assessment of the likelihood of its actual occurrence is a crucial part of the Theory of Reasoned Action and its applicability to health risk decision making. Overall, the motivation to comply was greater than the subjective norm for all of the items except "have condoms handy" (virtually the same) and "no sex" (where the subjective norm is significantly greater than the motivation to comply).

Table 6.3: Measures of *Behavioral Intention* among male inmates (product of subjective norm and motivation to comply, average scores)

Item	Subjective Norm	Motivation to comply	Behavioral Intention
partner(s) get tested	6.5	8.0	60.2
use latex condoms	6.5	7.2	54.0
have condoms handy	6.8	6.7	53.1
get tested for HIV	5.7	6.6	50.5
partner(s) "safer sex"	6.0	7.6	46.1
buy latex condoms	4.9	6.9	41.0
discuss "safer sex"	5.6	7.6	37.7
no Sex	5.1	3.3	23.9

Table 6.4 examines the perceived barriers to risk protection. Released offenders rated buying condoms and discussing condom use with their partner(s) as relatively easy. The perceived barriers increased with using condoms for a "one night stand" and discussing safe sex in a nonsexual setting, and making safe sex exciting. Offenders perceived the greatest barriers in avoiding alcohol/drugs if having sex later and using condoms if under the influence of alcohol/drugs.

Table 6.4: "Perceived Barriers" to risk protection among male offenders (ranked average scores where 10= "Very Hard" and 0= "Very Easy")

Behavior	average score
buy condoms	0.3
discuss condom use with partner(s)	0.6
use condoms for "one night stand"	0.9
discuss "safe sex" in nonsexual setting	1.0
make "safe sex" sexually exciting	1.2
avoid alcohol/drugs if having sex later	3.3
use condom if under influence alcohol/drugs	6.0

average total barriers score= 13.3
standard deviation= 9.0

TESTS OF HYPOTHESES

Table 6.5 presents the correlations, means, and standard deviations among the study variables for the 17 released male offenders. Examining the bivariate relationships reveals, consistent with the hypothesized relationships (Table 3.1), that HIV risk behaviors among released offenders is positively correlated with past alcohol/drug use (H1 r=.24); negatively correlated with knowledge about HIV/AIDS risk prevention (H3 r=-.34); and negatively correlated with behavioral intention to avoid specific HIV/AIDS risks (H4 r=-.11). However, contrary to the hypotheses, HIV risk behaviors among released offenders is positively correlated with supportive relationships (H2 r=.11); and negatively correlated with perceived barriers to specific HIV/AIDS risk avoidance (H5 r=-.34).

Younger offenders scored significantly higher on both the alcohol/drug history and HIV risk history measures. The alcohol/drug history scores were significantly related to the HIV risk history scores. Higher alcohol/drug scores were correlated with shorter periods of incarceration and higher levels of education were significantly related to higher scores on the HIV knowledge test and more "safer sex" behaviors during post-release. Those with less education perceived more barriers to safer sex. And paradoxically, those with greater social support also perceived more barriers to safer sex practices.

Table 6.5: Correlations, Means, and Standard Deviations of Study Variables

	1	2	3	4	5	6	7	8	9	10	11
x	38.9	10.5	4.9	42.6	52.5	2.5	22.2	352	13.3	11.9	8.6
sd	6.4	2.8	2.0	24.5	43.5	2.6	2.6	206	9.0	9.4	8.4
1		-.02	-.50*	-.52*	.42*	-.11	-.35	.08	.08	-.27	-.02
2			-.02	-.05	.10	.08	.74***	-.23	-.43*	-.51*	-.02
3				.72***	-.33	.05	.22	-.14	-.40	.09	.39
4					-.66**	.38	.29	-.05	-.15	.22	.24
5						-.16	-.24	.36	-.19	-.11	-.10
6							.15	-.08	.45*	-.40	.11
7								-.13	-.23	-.36	-.34
8									-.11	.19	-.11
9										-.18	-.34
10											-.09

1. age
2. years education
3. HIV risk history score
4. alcohol/drug score
5. months incarcerated
6. social support
7. HIV knowledge
8. behavioral intention
9. perceived barriers
10. safe behavior post-release
11. risk behavior post-release

*p<.05 **p<.01 ***p<.001 (one-tailed significance)

The robust statistical modeling technique of multiple regression analysis with Ordinary Least Squares (OLS) estimation (which attempts to maximize the coefficient of determination), was used to calculate post-release health-related behaviors. After controlling for the influences of age, education, HIV risk history, alcohol/drug history, months incarcerated, social supports, HIV knowledge, behavioral intention, and perceived barriers, one model predicted safer health behaviors and another predicted HIV risk behaviors.

Table 6.6: Multiple Regression Models Predicting Reentry Health-Related Behaviors (standardized coefficients in parenthesis)

	Safe Behavior	Risk Behavior
age	-1.04 (-.57)*	-6.49 (-.04)
education	-2.00 (-.53)	2.21 (.65)
HIV risk history	-2.23 (-.45)	2.73 (.62)
alcohol/drug history	.36 (.86)	-.21 (-.57)
months incarcerated	5.68 (.24)	-.13 (-.62)
social supports	-1.86 (-.52)	1.63 (.51)
HIV knowledge	-.82 (-.23)	-3.79 (-1.20)*
behavioral intention	-3.11 (-.07)	8.47 (.21)
perceived barriers	.13 (.12)	-.40 (-.41)
constant	86.0*	72.7
R square	.80	.74

*p<.05

As seen in Table 6.6, after controlling for the effects of other variables, the younger offenders were significantly more likely to engage in safer sex behaviors, and those with greater knowledge about HIV/AIDS were significantly less likely to engage in HIV risk behaviors. This analysis does not provide support for the cumulative effect (H6) of hypotheses 1-5. This shall be discussed in the final chapter.

7

Discussion and Conclusion

This study highlights the HIV prevention opportunities available within the context of offender release and reentry. It illustrates the value of approaching release from incarceration and reentry back inside the community as a troublesome period of transition, The challenges of reestablishing a productive life with a criminal record are formidable when one lacks family and community support systems. HIV avoidance would probably assume a higher priority for offenders who face the immediate concerns of housing, employment, and providing for families if greater support mechanisms were available.

This project also provides a better understanding of the difficulties and limitations of conducting research on offender populations. While the present sample of offenders shared many demographic characteristics with the broader offender population, representativeness cannot be demonstrated. Therefore, these results should be considered with caution. The data collection instruments used in this study have proved reliable in similar offender populations, but no attempt was made to verify the self-reported information. In addition, sample attrition has an undetermined impact on the results.

DIFFICULTIES AND LIMITATIONS

In research exploring sensitive subjects like drug use and sexual behavior, the validity of responses is a primary concern. One method that has been used successfully with incarcerated populations is to ask the respondent "if they know about (the type of behavior or activity)" as opposed to asking "if you have (engaged in the type of behavior or activity)." In addition, a particular time frame for the type of behavior or activity must be specified (e.g., within the last month).

Another concern is interviewer reactivity. I conducted all interviews. However, some inmates may have regarded me as an "outsider." This was mitigated by my previous experience in working with offenders at both adult and juvenile facilities. It is worth mentioning that being locked inside a small room with a person who is more comfortable in that setting than you are can be unsettling. During one interview, an inmate appeared to be hearing voices and was gesturing as if he was conversing back. I do not know if he was hallucinating or performing for me, but I decided that his interview data was not valid.

In another instance, I arranged to meet a released offender for lunch that I agreed to buy. After doing this several times, I decided that it was unproductive to be asking for responses when someone had their mouth full of food. Later, I began to arrange meetings in parking lots of restaurants. The first attempt was a disaster. We exchanged glances, hesitant to engage one another, for over 25 minutes. I was holding a clipboard, certainly anyone would know that it was I the researcher!

I never asked the offenders about their offenses. I kept my inquiries to the questionnaires. Yet, I listened when someone wanted to talk about other things. I met one of the released females in a restaurant parking lot on a cold and rainy afternoon. We decided to sit in my vehicle for the interview. Half way into the interview, she began to provide a rather detailed account of her sexual encounters inside the women's prison. This transpired for an uncomfortable period of time, until I suddenly noticed that all of the windows were completely fogged up.

At no time did I feel threatened or unsafe conducting this study. The logistical considerations of conducting interviews at two pre-release facilities and at a multitude of post-release locations while maintaining full teaching responsibilities at the university were demanding. As with anyone who has done government grant research, the administrative-bureaucratic apparatus must be mastered whether it be at the National Institutes of Health, the Delaware Department of Corrections, or Delaware State University. Fortunately, I found helpful individuals ready to assist.

DISCUSSION

The primary purpose of correctional institutions is custodial so support services are relegated a lower priority. Despite being housed in pre-release units, offenders expressed little, if any, advance knowledge of their actual day of release. Most were unable to say goodbye to long-time friends. One offender had no way of documenting his identity which delayed his applications for employment.

Offenders who did not "max out" their sentences moved from prison to a highly regimented work-release setting, where security demands limited their choices. Several subjects described the work-release center as more regimented than prison. Many released offenders lacked adequate educational, vocational, and decision making skills required for time and money management. Well-designed and properly-timed service delivery is imperative to an offender's successful release and reentry.

Offenders anticipated that "life moves faster on the outside" and several released offenders were anxious to "catch up" (including with intimate partners). Some exhibited little patience and much frustration in dealing with bureaucratic delays. Yet all clearly expressed the desire and motivation to accomplish life goals.

This study reveals that many inmates still engaged in risky behavior despite demonstrating knowledge of the health risks associated with HIV/AIDS. Health concerns were seen as distinct from preventative health issues. Protecting one's health was seen as a remote concern. Inmates learned in the prison environment that health care was not taken seriously (see Williams 2007).

Several shortcomings with the Reasoned Action approach are evident in this study. Consistent with "rational choice" models, Reasoned Action assumes that individuals possess equal cognitive abilities to make logical decisions, unimpeded by emotional states of mind. In addition, the impact of alcohol/drugs to impair decision making is ignored. Offenders in this study judged alcohol and drugs as significant barriers to HIV risk protection.

Reasoned Action overemphasizes individual choice and overlooks social factors that structure behavioral options. Rational choice models may be better suited for explaining behaviors among groups who do not interact in environments characterized by high rates of unemployment, single parenting, crime, and victimization. This does not excuse criminal behavior.

The high incarceration rates of minority group men skews the age-sex ratio in many communities. The removal of so many adult males from impoverished neighborhoods for such prolonged periods further disrupts the social structure of neighborhoods. Several released offenders spoke of the ready availability of multiple sex partners when they returned home. This had a destabilizing effect on monogamous ties. Appropriate male role models are lacking in many neighborhoods.

Further research is needed to address why the cumulative effects (H6) of the hypothetical relationships were not supported. Additional research is needed to examine why those with greater social support perceive more barriers to safer sex practices. We must explore the manner in which the influence of subjective norms can be bolstered so they exert a greater impact on the behavioral intention to avoid health risk behavior.

Those without strong social supports did not perceive the influence of subjective norms in ways that impacted behavior. More elaborate measures of social support are therefore required. Different kinds of support-emotional, physical, financial-would provide a variety of assistance to help offenders in protecting and maintaining their health and the health of their communities. Although the effect of attending religious service on HIV risk behaviors was not demonstrated in this study, Reasoned Action largely disregards the role of individual morality on decision making.

Research has shown that released offenders are vulnerable to health-related risks, and are at an increased risk for substance abuse and homelessness in the first days and weeks during the transition from incarceration. Successful HIV/AIDS prevention efforts must address the multiple priorities among released offenders. An individualized case management approach to offender reentry may maximize the perceived influence of significant others on individuals' behavioral intention regarding risk-taking.

ASSISTANCE THAT OFFENDERS WOULD LIKE TO SEE

Interview subjects were queried for ideas concerning HIV risk reduction follow-up programs. Eleven of the released male offenders and all of the females stated that they would be interested in participating if such a program were offered.[1] The majority of subjects felt that a "health assistance" program should be offered weekly. Most felt that such a program would last from 1–2 hours and be offered in the early evening at a community center.

According to the interview subjects, a program would include workshops, video presentations, guest speakers, HIV testing/counseling, and risk prevention mentors. Incentives to attend would include food, refreshments, and certificates of attendance. Working with community leaders and a community newsletter would be effective ways to let people know about the program(s).

An offender reentry/transition case management model is currently being designed. This project proposes an offender community reentry pilot program that will address fragmented service delivery by focusing on discharge planning and transitional case management. The intervention will provide needed support from the pre-release setting throughout the critical transition period and promote risk reduction behaviors post-release.

The proposal includes the following aims: 1) Design and implement a culturally-sensitive community reentry case management pilot program for released offenders and their families who are at-risk for HIV transmission; 2) Foster a continuum of services between public health providers, Delaware Department of Corrections (DDOC), and community-based organizations (CBOs); and 3) Evaluate the pilot program for wider implementation.

---

1. Three male subjects gave the following reasons for why they would NOT be interested in a follow-up program: "Doesn't pertain to me, pretty much already know what to do"; "Other priorities"; "Too busy, burned out on groups."

The transitional case management approach to service delivery has bridged the gap between public health providers, community based organizations, and client populations who are at risk. Case management can enhance 1) the continuity of care; 2) accessibility, by overcoming administrative/institutional barriers; 3) efficiency, by increasing the likelihood of a client receiving timely delivery of appropriate services; and 4) accountability. The key to discharge planning and case management is the coordination of care throughout the transitional period.

Several noteworthy interventions have helped reduce/prevent HIV transmission among released offenders by utilizing transitional case management. The Corrections Demonstration Project is a network of community projects that operates in seven states. The purpose of the project is to develop model programs that increase the collaboration among public health departments, correctional facilities, and community-based organizations in order to enhance prevention and care services to incarcerated persons at high-risk for HIV or living with HIV/AIDS. The objectives are to expand HIV-related services to inmates in correctional facilities and especially to those in the process of preparing for release or recently released from prisons, jails, and juvenile facilities.

Other examples of innovative interventions to enhance the continuity of HIV/AIDS care across the incarceration-community transition are the Massachusetts Transitional Intervention Program, the Homebase Project in California, New Jersey's grants to seven community-based HIV agencies, and New York's Hunter College Health Link Model. Service providers have helped released offenders to stay healthy and stay out of jail/prison by personally connecting with inmates prior to release. The prevention case management component of the program provides five months of intensive transitional support. This includes one-on-one client-centered case management, development of individual risk assessment and reduction action plans, and post release support through referrals to community-based agencies. A new pilot project utilizes a more comprehensive approach to transitional planning and includes case managers working with the inmate and his/her partner and family before and after release.

The Aids Risk Reduction Model provides a theoretical framework for the case management approach. It maintains that in order to change behavior, the behavior must first be seen as risky. This is followed by a commitment to change the behavior, and then by action taken to perform the desired change. Therefore, a pilot project utilizing discharge planning and transitional case management is being proposed for incarcerated minority members who are within six months of release from prison and who are at risk of HIV transmission.

CONCLUSION

This research project provides valuable information that illustrates that many of the difficulties released offenders encounter are inversely related to the availability of a support network, thus presenting a viable opportunity for intervention. This study reveals that many inmates still engage in risky behavior despite being knowledgeable about the health risks associated with HIV/AIDS. Current health problems are seen as distinct from preventative health issues. Therefore, protecting one's health may be a more remote concern among those who are faced with the immediate concerns of employment, housing, and having to provide for a family.

This study of offenders who are "trying to do good" hardly approaches the scope of the problems discussed in Chapter Two. The significant correlation between rates of incarceration and rates of HIV/AIDS cannot prove that one causes the other. But further research can refine the important factors to consider depending on the level of analysis. The problems that offenders encounter in Delaware and the US may pale in relation to those in other regions of the globe.

The destabilizing effect that the "incarceration binge fueled by the war on drugs" has on neighborhoods, communities, and cities, is also seen internationally with the impact of HIV/AIDS. Nations and regions of the globe are losing entire generations of people who would have been socially and economically productive. Ultimately this may have a similar destabilizing effect on political stability around the world.

Foremost, our policymakers must "try to do good" by tackling the problems associated with mandatory minimum sentencing and privatized prison health care. Programs structured for bureaucratic expedience must be redesigned. Research has shown that HIV transmission inside prisons is greater where inmates serve longer terms, our policymakers must advocate therapeutic justice and successful alternatives to incarceration.

Adapting a HIV prevention intervention model for inmate pre-release programs has to address fragmented service delivery by focusing on discharge planning and transitional case management. Interventions should provide needed support from the pre-release setting throughout the critical release/reentry period and promote risk reduction behaviors post release. Future research should examine the impact that a transitional case management approach to service delivery would make to the long-term goal of reducing HIV risk behaviors.

Appendix A

State of Delaware Department of Corrections Profile of
Inmate Population 2005

DDC is the only government operated correction agency in the state of
Delaware, supervising 6,530 inmates in its facilities and over 20,000 probationers in the community (a 30% increase in the last three years according to the Delaware Statistical Analysis Center). Racial and ethnic
minority groups are over-represented in the Delaware inmate population.

Overcrowding in Delaware Corrections:

Correction Facility	Design Capacity	Avg. daily population
DCC	3,131	5,100
BOP	2,731	4,650
Half-way	400	450

The average length of stay for:

detention	97.8 days
jail	93.8 days
prison	30.7 months
life	9.0 years
death	5.2 years

Distribution of HIV symptomatic inmates in Delaware (Prison Health Services 6/30/99):

DCC Facility	# inmates HIV symptomatic	and taking medications
Baylor	24	13
DCC	62	51
Gander Hill	46	41
Morris	1	1
Plummer	2	2
SussexWR	7	7
SCI	15	10
Webb	2	2
Total	159	127

Appendix B

Informed Consent Signature Form

Project Director: Dr. Lee Streetman
Title of Project: Health Risk Behavior Decision-Making Among Inmates Communities

You are invited to participate in an interview at this correctional facility. Your participation is valuable, but totally voluntary and confidential. This is important research about health behavior decision-making. Your honesty goes a long way in helping us to understand the important factors to consider. Before you sign this form, you are welcome to ask questions, now or later, by contacting Dr. Lee Streetman. If at any time you have questions concerning your rights as a research subject, you may contact the Office of Sponsored Programs at Delaware State University.

This form will be kept in a locked file cabinet located at Delaware State University where access will be limited to the research team. I have read all items on the Information Sheet, and all my questions have been answered. I understand the following:

- my participation is voluntary;

- my name does not appear on interview or other data collection forms, only a code number will be used;

- my participation or decision not to do an interview will not result in any penalty for me;

- I can discontinue participation at any time without penalty; and

- all information will be kept in a locked metal file cabinet and will only be available to the study research staff; it will not be shared with any DOC staff members or other persons in DOC facilities.

YOU ARE MAKING A DECISION WHETHER OR NOT TO PARTICIPATE. YOUR SIGNATURE INDICATES THAT YOU HAVE DECIDED TO PARTICIPATE, HAVING BEEN READ THE INFORMATION PROVIDED ABOVE.

Participant's ID number:_____

Participant's Signature: _____ Date: / /

Interviewer's Signature: _____ Date: / /

Code number: _____

Appendix C

Data Collection Instruments

The present research adapted two data collection instruments to the research sites (DCC and MPCJF): the Goal Attainment/Functional Status Assessment (Rapkin et al. 1994) and the Information, Motivation, and Behavioral Skills (IMB) Interview (Misovich et al. 1998). The IMB model of AIDS risk behavior change has been developed and validated to serve as general conceptualization for understanding and promoting AIDS risk reduction behavior change. The questionnaire takes approximately 45 minutes to complete when used in a university student population and includes the following sections: Demographic Measures, AIDS Prevention Information Measures, Measures of Motivation to Perform AIDS Preventive Behavior, Attitudes toward AIDS preventive acts, Subjective norms regarding AIDS preventive acts, Behavioral intentions for AIDS prevention, Behavioral skills measures, AIDS Preventive Behaviors.

GOAL ATTAINMENT INTERVIEW

I. INTRODUCTION:
Now that the outlook for people with HIV is changing, we're interested in how people are thinking about the future and what they're hoping to do. What are some things you'd like to accomplish?

1.

2.

3.

4.

II. TIME FRAME: Do you see this happening in the coming year or some time after that?

1. First goal _____ coming year _____ future year

2. Second goal _____ coming year _____ future year

3. Third goal _____ coming year _____ future year

4. Fourth goal _____ coming year _____ future year

III. ACTION:

Have you begun to take steps to make this happen?

1.

2.

3.

4.

IV. SELF-EFFICACY

On a scale of 1-10, how confident are you that this is going to happen?

1.

2.

3.

HEALTH AND RELATIONSHIP SURVEY

Please answer each question below by circling a number to its right, according to this scale:

1=Strongly Agree,   2=Agree Somewhat,   3=Neither Agree nor Disagree,
            4=Disagree Somewhat,   5=Strongly Disagree

1. More of the virus that causes AIDS is found in blood and semen than in other body fluids.

2. It is estimated that more than one million Americans are currently infected with the virus that causes AIDS.

HEALTH AND RELATIONSHIP SURVEY (continued)

3. If you do not use condoms, withdrawal of the penis immediately before orgasm reduces the risk of getting the virus that causes AIDS to the point where it is highly unlikely that a person will get it.

4. A person is not very likely to get AIDS by sharing IV-drug needles with someone who has the virus.

5. These days, it is very unlikely that a blood transfusion would give a person the virus that causes AIDS.

6. Unprotected oral sex is less risky for transmitting the virus that causes AIDS than unprotected vaginal sex.

7. Most people who have been exposed to the virus that causes AIDS show clearly visible symptoms of serious illness.

8. The virus that causes AIDS is not spread by sneezing or coughing.

9. There are no cases of people getting the virus that causes AIDS from contact with saliva.

10. A person can be infected with the virus that causes AIDS for five or more years without developing AIDS.

11. Several people have gotten the virus that causes AIDS by donating blood.

12. It is unsafe to use drinking fountains or public toilets that might have been used by somebody who has the virus that causes AIDS.

13. Some people have gotten the virus that causes AIDS from infected people's sweat in gymnasiums or health clubs.

14. If you kiss someone who has the virus that causes AIDS, who will probably get the disease.

15. A woman who is infected with the virus that causes AIDS cannot pass the disease to her infant.

16. The virus that causes AIDS is not spread by mosquitoes.

17. Through sexual intercourse, men can transmit the virus that causes AIDS somewhat more easily to women than women can to men.

HEALTH AND RELATIONSHIP SURVEY (continued)

18. Oil-based lubricants such as Vaseline should be used to lubricate condoms.

19. Condoms may be safely stored in one's wallet for up to two months.

20. In order for a condom to effectively reduce one's risk for the virus that causes AIDS, it must be put on before any sexual intercourse takes place.

21. Natural condoms made of animal products are as effective as latex condoms in preventing the virus that causes AIDS.

22. Medical experts believe that most people infected with the virus that causes AIDS will eventually develop AIDS.

23. In order for the virus that causes AIDS to be transmitted from one person to another, there must be direct contact between one person's blood, vaginal excretions or semen, and the other person's blood.

24. Condoms have an "expiration date" like food does, and you should not buy condoms whose expiration date has passed.

25. Nonoxynol-9 (found in some spermicides and foams) has been shown to kill the virus that causes AIDS.

26. If you have "confidential" HIV blood test, you have to give your name to the testing site.

27. People can get the virus that causes AIDS be eating food that has been prepared by someone who has the disease.

28. Children who have the virus that causes AIDS can easily spread the disease to other children.

29. It is unsafe to share drinking glasses and eating utensils with people who have the virus that causes AIDS.

30. Many health-care workers have become infected as a result of treating AIDS patients.

31. Household pets can spread the virus that causes AIDS to people.

HEALTH AND RELATIONSHIP SURVEY (continued)

32. If a person has unsafe sex and an HIV blood test two weeks later indicates that they do not have the virus that causes AIDS, they can be fairly certain that they were not exposed to the AIDS virus.

33. When properly used, latex condoms greatly reduce the chance that the virus that causes AIDS will be transmitted through sexual intercourse.

34. According to a recent study, about 1 in 500 college students have been exposed to the virus that causes AIDS.

35. There are several locations on campus where condoms can be purchased at any hour of the night.

36. Most college students who get infected with the virus that causes AIDS during college will feel fine and show no symptoms of AIDS throughout their college career.

37. Condoms may be purchased at the Student Infirmary, and charged to your next semester's fee bill.

38. If you know a person's sexual history and lifestyle before you have sex with them, it is unnecessary to use condoms.

39. The way a person behaves around you when you first meet them is probably a good indicator of whether or not they are the type of person who may have been exposed to the virus that causes AIDS.

40. You really only need to use condoms during "one night stands."

41. You can tell whether a potential sex partner is at risk for AIDS by how they dress and how they look.

42. When you feel you have gotten to know someone very well, you no longer need to practice safer sex with them.

43. Asking you partner about their sexual history is a good way to find out whether or not to practice safer sex with them.

44. As long as a person doesn't belong to a "high risk" group such as gays or drug users, you really don't need to worry about getting the virus that causes AIDS from them.

HEALTH AND RELATIONSHIP SURVEY (continued)

45. If two people have sex only with each other, they really don't have to practice safer sex.

46. Individuals in urban areas should definitely follow safer-sex guidelines, but individuals in rural areas really don't need to.

Each question below is asked in the context of what you would think or do *in the next month*. Although many of the situations discussed might be relevant for a much longer period of time, for research purposes, we need to have a standard time frame.

Answer each of the questions below by putting an X on the part of the line that best represents your feelings. Be sure to put your mark *within one of the five intervals on each line*.

For example, if your answer to a question below was "very good," "somewhat nice," and "neither pleasant nor unpleasant" your response would like this:

My getting a new car during the next month would be:

very good		X						very bad
very awful					X			very nice
very pleasant				X				very unpleasant

The questions below deal with not having sexual intercourse at all.

Note: When we say "sexual intercourse," we mean sex where the penis is put into the vagina or sex where the penis is put into the rectum (the behind).

1. My not having sexual intercourse at all during the next month would be:

2. Most people who are important to me think that I should not have sexual intercourse at all during the next month.

very true | | | | | | | | very untrue

HEALTH AND RELATIONSHIP SURVEY (continued)

3. I intend to not have sexual intercourse at all during the next month.
   very likely |___|___|___|___|___| very unlikely

Please Note:
Many of the questions in this section ask you to describe your feelings about a specific behavior that involves a sexual partner. If you do not currently have a sexual partner, please answer those questions as *if you had a sexual partner*.

The questions below deal with discussing safer sex with sexual partners.

4. My talking about safer sex (how to keep from getting the virus that causes AIDS) with my sexual partner(s) before having sex with them during the next month would be:

5. Most people who are important to me think I should talk about safer sex with my partner(s) before having sex with them during the next month.
   very true |___|___|___|___|___| very untrue

6. If I have sex during the next month, I intend to talk about safer sex with my partner(s) before having sex with them.
   very likely |___|___|___|___|___| very unlikely

The questions below deal with trying to persuade your partner(s) to practice only safer sex.

7. Trying to persuade my partner(s) to practice only safer sex (for example, to use latex condoms) during the next month would be:

8. Most people who are important to me think I should try to persuade my partner(s) to practice only safer sex during the next month.
   very true |___|___|___|___|___| very untrue

9. If I have sex during the next month, I intend to try to persuade my partner(s) to practice only safer sex.
   very likely |___|___|___|___|___| very unlikely

HEALTH AND RELATIONSHIP SURVEY (continued)

The questions below deal with buying latex condoms.

10. My buying latex condoms during the next month would be:

11. Most people who are important to me think I should buy latex condoms during the next month.

    very true | | | | | | | very untrue

12. I intend to buy latex condoms during the next month.

    very likely | | | | | | | very unlikely

The next questions deal with always making sure you have latex condoms handy.

13. Always having latex condoms handy during the next month would be:

14. Most people who are important to me think I should always have latex condoms handy during the next month.

    very true | | | | | | | very untrue

15. I intend to always have latex condoms handy during the next month.

    very likely | | | | | | | very unlikely

The questions below deal with always using latex condoms during sexual intercourse

16. In the next month, my partner(s) and I always using latex condoms during sexual intercourse would be:

17. Most people who are important to me think my partner(s) and I should always use latex condoms during sexual intercourse in the next month.

    very true | | | | | | | very untrue

18. If I have sexual intercourse during the next month, I intend to have my partner(s) and I always use latex condoms.

    very likely | | | | | | | very unlikely

HEALTH AND RELATIONSHIP SURVEY (continued)

The questions below are about getting a blood test for the virus that causes AIDS.

19. Getting a blood test during the next month to check whether I have the virus that causes AIDS would be:

20. Most people who are important to me think I should get a blood test during the next month to check whether I have the virus that causes AIDS.

    very likely |___|___|___|___|___|___| very untrue

21. I intend to get a blood test during the next month to check whether I have the virus that causes AIDS.

    very likely |___|___|___|___|___|___| very unlikely

The questions below deal with asking your partner to get a blood test for the virus that causes AIDS.

22. Asking my partner(s) to get a blood test during the next month to check whether they have the virus that causes AIDS would be:

23. Most people who are important to me think I should ask my partner(s) to get a blood test during the next month to check whether they have the virus that causes AIDS.

    very likely |___|___|___|___|___|___| very unlikely

24. I intend to ask my partner(s) to get a blood test during the next month to check whether they have the virus that causes AIDS.

    very likely |___|___|___|___|___|___| very untrue

For the following questions, please circle the answer you feel best applies to you. We realize some of these questions may seem a bit repetitive or awkward, but for scientific reasons, the questions have to be phrased in a particular way. Each of the questions is different, and each is important to the outcome of this study. Please be patient and answer as best you can.

Please circle how *hard or easy* it would be for you to do each of the following things.

HEALTH AND RELATIONSHIP SURVEY (continued)

1. How hard would it be for you to buy condoms?

2. How hard would it be for you to be supportive if your sexual partner brought up the topic of using condoms to reduce the risk of getting the virus that causes AIDS?

3. How hard would it be for you to make *safer* sex with a latex condom sexually exciting for your partner?

4. How hard would it be for you to discuss safer sex (for example, always using latex condoms) with your partner in a nonsexual setting, such as riding in your car?

5. How hard would it be for you to consistently use condoms with a partner *every time* you have a one-night stand?

6. How hard would it be for you to use a condom with your partner while under the influence of alcohol or drugs?

7. How hard would it be for you to avoid using alcohol or drugs if you think you might be having sex later?

Please circle how *effectively or ineffectively* you feel you could do each of the following things.

8. How effectively could you discuss safer sex (such as using latex condoms) with your partner before having sex with them?

9. How effectively could you refuse to have unsafe sexual intercourse? (Note: unsafe sexual intercourse means (1) penis-in-vagina intercourse, no condom; or (2) penis-in-rectum intercourse, no condom).

10. If you were about to have sex, how effectively could you show your partner nonverbally (for example, through body movements) that you want to practice only safer sex?

11. How effectively could you tell your partner through a joke of a "one-liner" that you want to practice only safer sex?

HEALTH AND RELATIONSHIP SURVEY (continued)

12. How effectively could you convince your partner to practice only safer sex?

13. How effectively could you convince your partner to use a condom for *vaginal* sex?

14. How effectively could you convince your partner to use a condom (or other latex barrier) for *oral* sex?

15. How effectively could you plan ahead to be sure you always have condoms on hand whenever you have sex?

16. How effectively could you make safer sex (using a latex condom) enjoyable for your partner?

17. How effectively could you make your partner feel good about using condoms during *vaginal intercourse*?

18. How effectively could you make your partner feel good about using condoms (or another latex barrier) during *oral sex*?

19. How effectively could you refuse to have *oral sex* without a condom or other latex barrier?

For the items below, we want you to answer as if you were *currently in a long-term relationship*, in which you have been having intercourse *without* using condoms (e.g., if you or your partner are using birth control pills).

20. How effectively could you discuss initiating safer sexual practices (e.g., using a latex condom) with your partner?

21. How effectively could you persuade your partner to begin practicing only safer sex (sex with a latex condom) with you?

22. If you were able to persuade your partner to begin using latex condoms with you, how hard would it be for you to continue using condoms *every time* you have sexual intercourse until both of you get a HIV blood test?

23. How effectively could you persuade your partner to get an HIV blood test with you?

HEALTH AND RELATIONSHIP SURVEY (continued)

For the items below, we want you to answer as if you were *currently in a long-term relationship*, in which you have been having sexual intercourse *with* a condom.

24. How effectively could you persuade your partner to continue to use condoms with you *every time* you have sexual intercourse?

25. How hard would it be for you to continue using condoms with your partner *every time* you have sexual intercourse until both of you get an HIV blood test?

Imagine that you are in your room with an attractive person whom you have recently met and you like very much. It is clear from their behavior that they want to have sexual intercourse with you, and you also want to have sex with them. However, when you have sex you want you and your partner to use a condom to reduce both of your risk of becoming infected with the virus that causes AIDS.

26. How effectively could you discuss safer sexual practices with this new partner before having sex with them?

27. How effectively could you persuade them to practice only safer sex (sex with a condom) with you?

28. If you were about to have sex, how effectively could you show them nonverbally (for example, through body movements) that you want to practice only safer sex?

29. How effectively could you tell them through a joke or a "one-liner" that you want to practice only safer sex?

30. How effectively do you think you could use a condom without discussing it at all with them, by just putting it on before sex?

31. Overall, how effectively could you make sure that a condom is used?

32. If no condom is available, instead of having intercourse, how hard would it be for you to engage in another pleasurable activity (such as mutual masturbation) where a condom isn't needed?

HEALTH AND RELATIONSHIP SURVEY (continued)

33. If no condom is available, how hard would it be for you to stop sexual activity while you or your partner go to get a condom?

Now imagine that your attractive partner who you've recently met says that using a condom is unnecessary, because one of you is on the pill. You still want to use a condom because of your concerns about getting the virus that causes AIDS.

34. How effectively do you think you could convince this partner that the two of you should use a condom, without making them refuse to have sex with you?

35. How effectively do you think you could negotiate a safer sexual alternative with them? For instance, if they refused to use a condom, how effectively could you convince them to engage in another sexual activity, such as mutual masturbation?

36. How hard would it be for you to refuse to have sex with them if they refused to use a condom with you?

We would like you to tell us whether you have done each of the following things during the time interval which is indicated.

1. Have you had *sexual intercourse* (sex in which the penis is put into the vagina, or sex where the penis is put into the rectum) at all during the past *month*? *Circle one*:

<table>
<tr><td>Yes: I have had sexual intercourse during the past month.</td><td>No: I have not had sexual intercourse during the past month.</td></tr>
</table>

2. Have you ever had sexual intercourse during your lifetime? *Circle one*:   Yes   No

3. Please circle *any* of the alternatives below that apply to both you and your sexual partner(s) during the past *month*.

A. Both I and all my sexual partners have tested HIV negative.

HEALTH AND RELATIONSHIP SURVEY (continued)

B. Both I and my sexual partner have never had any other sexual partners.

C. Neither of the above are true for me and my partner(s) during the past month.

D. I have not had any sexual partners during the past month.

4. Are you in a close relationship involving sexual intercourse?
   Circle one: Yes   No

5. If you answered "Yes" to number 4 (above), is your relationship with your partner monogamous (neither of you has sexual intercourse with other people)?
   Circle one: Yes   No   Uncertain   Not applicable: I was not in a
   sexual relationship.

6. I have discussed safer sex with a sexual partner (or sexual partners) before having sex with them during the past *month*.
   Circle one: Yes   No   Not applicable: I have not had sexual inter-
   course during the past month.

7. I have bought latex condoms some place nearby where they were easily available during the past *month*.
   Circle one: Often   A few times   Once   Never

8. I kept latex condoms some place where they were easily available during the past month.
   Circle one: Always   Often   Sometimes   Rarely   Never

9. My partner(s) and I have used latex condoms when having sexual intercourse (sex in which the penis is put into the vagina, or sex in which the penis is put into the rectum) during the past *month*.
   Circle one:

   Never   Rarely   Sometimes   Often   Always   Not applicable: I have
   not had sexual inter-
   course during the
   past month.

   <u>Fill in Number Below</u>

HEALTH AND RELATIONSHIP SURVEY (continued)

10. How many different people have you had vaginal intercourse (penis-in-vagina) with during the last month?

11. With how many of these partners were condoms used all the time?

12. How many of these partners had an AIDS blood test and you knew they had not been exposed to the virus that causes AIDS?

13. When you had *vaginal intercourse* during the past *month*, how often were condoms used?
    Circle one:
    Never   Rarely   Sometimes   Often   Always   Not applicable: I have not had sexual inter-course during the past month.

14. When you had vaginal intercourse during the past month, what percentage of the time were condoms used?
    _____%   Not applicable: I have not had vaginal intercourse during the past month.

15. How many different people have you had *anal intercourse* (penis-in-rectum) during the last month?

16. With how many of these partners were condoms used all the time?

17. How many of these partners had an AIDS blood test and you knew they had not been exposed to the virus that causes AIDS?

18. When you had *anal intercourse* during the past *month*, how often were condoms used?
    Circle one:
    Never   Rarely   Sometimes   Often   Always   Not applicable: I have not had sexual inter-course during the past month.

HEALTH AND RELATIONSHIP SURVEY (continued)

19. I have tried to convince or persuade my sex partner(s) to practice only safer sex (always using condoms) during the past *month*.
Circle one:

Always	Sometimes	Never	Not applicable: I havenot had sex during the past month.	Does not apply: My partner has wanted to have only safer sex (always using a latex condom) during the past month.

20. Circle the letter which applies to you.

    A. I have sex only with men.

    B. I have sex with both men and women.

    C. I have sex only with women.

    D. I don't have sexual intercourse.

The following questions concern having a blood test to find out if you have been exposed to the virus that causes AIDS.

21. I have had a blood test to check whether I have been exposed to the virus that causes AIDS during the past month.
Circle one: Yes   No   Not applicable: I have never had sexual intercourse or used injection drugs.

22. I have made an appointment to get a blood test to check whether I have been exposed to the virus that causes AIDS during the past month.
Circle one: Yes   No   Not applicable: I have never had sexual intercourse or used injection drugs.

23. At some time in the past, I have had a blood test to determine whether I have been exposed to the virus that causes AIDS.
Circle one: Yes   No

24. If you had a blood test for the virus that causes AIDS, where did you have this blood test?

HEALTH AND RELATIONSHIP SURVEY (continued)

Circle the letter which applies to you:

A. Anonymous test site (you don't have to give your name)

B. Confidential test site (you give your name, but it is kept confidential)

C. Doctor's office

D. Through the military or ROTC

E. Blood donation

F. Other

Appendix D

Websites for Further Information

www.prisonstudies.org
International Centre for Prison Studies. King's College, University of London. International data on incarceration rates.

www.UNAIDS.org
Joint United Nations Programe on HIV/AIDS. International data on HIV/AIDS rates.

www.cdc.gov
Centers for Disease Control and Prevention. Most recent data and information on HIV/AIDS in the United States with subgroup comparisons.

www.ojp.usdoj.gov/bjs
Bureau of Justice Statistics. United States Department of Justice, Office of Justice Programs. Incarceration data at federal and state facilities.

http://doc.delaware.gov
Delaware Department of Corrections. Incarceration and community corrections data.

www.aidsdelaware.org
AIDS Delaware. HIV/AIDS data for state of Delaware.

www.delawarehiv.org
Delaware HIV Consortium. Volunteer groups to assist HIV/AIDS risk groups in Delaware.

www.surj.org
Stand Up for What's Right and Just. Policy reform non-profit organization in Delaware.

www.prisonsucks.org
Prison Policy Initiative. Criticism of current corrections policies.

References

ACE Program. (1998). *Breaking the Walls of Silence: AIDS and Women in a New York State Maximum Security Prison.* Woodstock, NY: Overlook Press.

Ajezen, I. and Fishbein, M. (1980). *Understanding attitudes and predicting social behavior.* Englewood Cliffs, NJ: Prentice Hall.

Arp III, W. (2004). HIV/AIDS and Nondecision in Louisiana. *Journal of Black Studies.* 34, 548-561.

Arthur, W. (1994). Inductive Reasoning and Bounded Rationality. *American Economic Review.* 84, 406-411.

Bachrach, P. and Baratz, M. (1962). *Power and Poverty.* New York: Oxford University Press.

Baker, J., Doe, J., Epstein, J., Hagans, T., Siers, B., Streetman, L., and Woodlin, H. (2001). *Needs Assessment, Resource Inventory, and Gap Analysis Report.* Delaware Division of Public Health and Delaware HIV Consortium.

Bandura, A. (1977). Social Learning Theory. Englewood Cliffs, NJ: Prentice-Hall.

Binswanger, I., Stern, M., Deyo, R., Heagerty, P., Cheadle, A., Elmore, J., and Koepsell, T. (2007). Release from Prison—A High Risk of Death for Former Inmates. *The New England Journal of Medicine,* 356, 157-165.

Boyd, R. and Richerson, P. (2002). Norms and Rationality. In G. Gigerenzer and R. Selten (Eds.), Bounded Rationality: The Adaptive Toolbox. Cambridge, MA: MIT Press.

Braithwaite, R., Hammett, T., and Mayberry, R. (1996). *Prisons and AIDS*. San Francisco, CA: Jossey-Bass.

Brettle, R. (1991). HIV and Harm Reduction for Injection Drug Users. *AIDS*, 5, 125-136.

Bureau of Justice Statistics. (2006). *Prison and Jail Inmates at Midyear 2005*. Washington, DC: US Department of Justice, Bureau of Justice Statistics Bulletin.

Catania, J., Kegeles, S., and Coates, T. (1990). Toward an Understanding of Risk Behavior: An AIDS Risk Reduction Model. *Health Education Quarterly* ,17, 53-72.

Carney, J., Werth, J., and Morris, R. (1997). AIDS-Related Knowledge and Beliefs Among Incarcerated Adolescent Males. *Criminal Justice and Behavior*, 24, 96-113.

Centers for Disease Control and Prevention. (2006). Twenty-five years of HIV/AIDS-United States, 1981-2006. *MMWR*, 55, 585-589.

Centers for Disease Control and Prevention. (2005). *HIV/AIDS Surveillance Report*. Atlanta: U.S. Department of Health and Human Services.

Centers for Disease Control & Prevention. (1998). Linking Science and Prevention Programs—The Need for Comprehensive Strategies. *National Center for HIV, STD & TB Prevention*.

Cohen, L. and Felson, M. (1979). Social Change and Crime Rate Trends: A Routine Activity Approach, *American Sociological Review*, 44, 588-608.

Comfort, M., Grinstead, O., Faigeles, B., and Zack, B. (2000). Reducing HIV Risk Among Women Visiting Their Incarcerated Male Partners. *Criminal Justice Behavior*, 27, 57-71.

DeJong, W., Finn, P., Grand, J., and Markoff, L. (1994). Relapse Prevention. Rockville, MD: National Institute on Drug Abuse.

Delaware Health and Social Services. (2005). *Delaware Epidemiological Profile 2004, HIV/AIDS Epidemiology Health Promotion & Disease Prevention.* Division of Public Health.

Delaware Statistical Analysis Center. (2006). *Crime in Delaware.* Dover, DE.

Dolan, K., Wodak, A., Hall, W., and Kaplan, E. (1998). "A Mathematical model of HIV transmission in NSW prisons." *Drug Alcohol Dependency,* 50(3), 197-202.

Fishbein, M. and Ajezen, I. (1975). *Belief, attitude, intention, and behavior.* Reading, MA: Addison-Wesley.

Foreman, F. (2003). Intimate Risk, Sexual Risk Behavior Among African American College Women. *Journal of Black Studies,* 33, 637-653.

Frisch, D., and Baron, J. (1988). Ambiguity and rationality. *Journal of Behavioral Decision Making,* 1, 149-157.

Gardner, M. and Steinberg, L. (2005). Peer Influence on Risk Taking, Risk Preference, and Risky Decision Making in Adolescence and Adulthood: An Experimental Study. *Developmental Psychology,* 41, 625-635.

Grinstead, O., Zack, B., Faigeles, B., Grossman, N., and Blea, L. (1999a). Reducing Postrelease HIV Risk Among Male Prison Inmates. *Criminal Justice and Behavior,* 26, 453-465.

Grinstead, O., Zack, B., and Faigeles, B. (1999b). Collaborative Research to Prevent HIV among Male Prison Inmates and their Female Partners. *Health Education & Behavior,* 26, 225-238.

Hallinan, J. (2001) *Going Up the River, Travels in a Prison Nation.* New York: Random House.

Hammett, T., Harmon, P., and Maruschak, L. (1999). *HIV/AIDS, STDs, and TB in Correctional Facilities.* National Institute of Justice: Bureau of Justice Statistics.

Inciardi, J., Martin, S., Butzin, C., Hooper, R., and Harrison, L. (1997). An Effective Model of Prison-Based Treatment for Drug-Involved Offenders. *Journal of Drug Issues,* 27, 261-278.

Inciardi, J., Lockwood, D., Martin, S., Pottieger, A., and Scarpitti, F. (1994). HIV Infection Among Delaware Prison Releasees. *The Prison Journal,* 74, 364-370.

International Centre for Prison Studies. (2000). *Annual Report.* Kings College, London, UK.

Jolofani, D. and DeGabriele, J. (2002). *HIV/AIDS in Malawi Prisons.* Penal Reform International.

Jurgens, R. (1999). HIV/AIDS in Prisons: Final Report. *Crime & Justice International,* 17, (Winter). Canadian HIV/AIDS Legal Network and Canadian AIDS Society: National AIDS Clearinghouse and Office of International Criminal Justice Inc.

Kalichman, S. (1998). *Preventing AIDS: A Sourcebook for Behavioral Interventions.* Mahwah, NJ: Lawrence Erlbaum Associates.

Kahn, S. (2000). "Fire in the Belly." *HIV Plus,* 6 (January).

Katz, J. (1980). *Seductions of Crime: Moral and Sensual Attractions in Doing Evil.* New York: Basic Books.

Krienert, J. and Fleisher, M. (2004). *Crime & Employment.* New York: AltaMira.

Laszlo, A. and Smith, B. (1991). Evaluating Criminal Justice Training Addressing AIDS Policy. *Crime & Delinquency,* 37, 19-35.

Levin, I., Hart, S., Weller, J., and Harshman, L. (in press). Stability of choices in a risky decision-making task: a 3-year longitudinal study with children and adults. *Journal of Behavioral Decision Making.*

MMWR. (1996). HIV/AIDS Education and Prevention Programs For Adults in Prisons and Jails and Juveniles in Confinement Facilities—United States, 1994. *MMWR Weekly.*

(1992). HIV Prevention in the U.S. Correctional System, 1991. *MMWR Weekly.*

Maddow, R. (2000). "In the Big House." *HIV Plus*, 6 (January).

Malkin, I. and R. Elliot. (1995). "Governments' Responsibility in Preventing Prisoners' Exposure to HIV in Prison." *Canadian HIV/AIDS Policy & Law Newsletter*, 2 (Oct.).

Mantell, J., DiVittis, A., and Auerbach, M. (1997). *Evaluating HIV Prevention Interventions.* New York: Plenum Press.

Marquart, J., Merianos, D., Herbert, J., and Carroll, L. (1997). Health Condition and Prisoners: A Review of Research and Emerging Areas of Inquiry. *The Prison Journal*, 77, 184-208.

Martin, R., Zimmerman, S., Long, B., and West, A. (1995). A Content Assessment and Comparative Analysis of Prison-Based AIDS Education Programs for Inmates. *The Prison Journal*, 75, 5-47.

Martin, R., Zimmerman, S., and Long, B. (1993). AIDS Education in U.S. Prison: A Survey of Inmate Programs. *The Prison Journal*, 73, 103-129.

Martin, S. and Inciardi, J. (1997). Case Management Outcomes for Drug-Involved Offenders. *The Prison Journal*, 77, 168-183.

Maruschak, L. (1999). "HIV in Prisons 1997." *Bureau of Justice Statistics.* November, NCJ 178284:1-12.

Misovich, S., Fisher, W., and Fisher, J. (1998). A Measure of AIDS Prevention Information, Motivation, Behavioral Skills, and Behavior. In *Handbook of Sexuality-Related Measures.* New York: Sage.

National Institutes of Health. (1997). *Interventions to Prevent HIV Risk Behaviors.* National Institutes of Health Consensus Development Program: Bethesda, MD.

(1995). Behavioral, Social Science, and Prevention Research Area Review Panel Findings & Recommendations. *NIH AIDS Research Program Evaluation.*

National Library of Medicine. (1994). Psychosocial Aspects of AIDS (CBM 97-7). *Current Bibliographies in Medicine,* National Library of Medicine, (PSD): Bethesda, MD.

Office of AIDS Research. (1997). HIV/AIDS-Related Research Program. *Office of AIDS Research, NIH:* Bethesda, MD.

Okigbo, C., Okigbo, C., Hall Jr., W. and Ziegler. (2002). The HIV/AIDS Epidemic in African American Communities, Lessons From UNAIDS and Africa. *Journal of Black Studies,* 32, 615-653.

Parra, E. and Williams, L. (2005). An AIDS epidemic is raging behind bars. *Wilmington News Journal,* Sept. 26: A1.

Pfeffer, J. (1981). *Power in Organizations.* Marshfield, MA: Pitman Publishing.

Peters, E., Vastfjall, D., Garling, T., and Slovic, P. (2006). Affect and decision making: a "hot" topic." *Journal of Behavioral Decision Making,* 19, 79-85.

Petersilia, J. (2003). *When Prisoners Come Home: Parole and Prisoner Reentry.* New York: Oxford University Press.

Prochaska, J., DiClemente, C., and Norcross, J. (1992). In Search of How People Change. *American Psychologist,* 47, 1102-1114.

Rapkin, B., Smith, M., Dumont, K., Correa, A., Palmer, S., and Cohen. S. (1994). Development of the Idiographic Functional Assessment: A Measure of the Personal Goals and Goal Attainment Activities of People with AIDS. *Psychology and Health,* 9, 111-129.

Richard, R., Van de Plight, J., and De Vries, N. (1998). Anticipated Regret and Time Perspective: Changing Sexual Risk-taking Behavior. *Journal of Behavioral Decision Making,* 9, 185-199.

Rosenstock, I., V. Strecher, and M. Becker. (1994). The Health Belief Model and HIV Risk Behavior Change. In R. DiClemente (ed.) *Preventing AIDS: Theories and Methods of Behavioral Intentions.* New York: Plenum Press.

Russo, J. and Schoemaker, P. (1989). Decision Traps. New York: Simon & Schuster.

Sampson, R. and Laub, J. (1993). *Crime in the Making: Pathways and turning points through life.* Cambridge, MA: Harvard University Press.

Saum, C., Surrat, H., Inciardi, J., and Bennett, R. (1995). Sex in Prison: Exploring the Myths and Realities. *The Prison Journal,* 75, 413-430.

Schedffer, M. and M. Marthe. (2000). "HIV/AIDS: An Epidemic Behind Bars" Panos Institute.

Schmid, T. and Jones, R. (1996). Suspended Identity: Transformation in a Maximum Security Prison. In D. Kelly (Ed.) *Deviant Behavior* (pp. 427-443). New York: St. Martins.

Shover, N. and Honaker, D. (1996). The Socially Bounded Decision Making of Persistent Property Offenders. In D. Kelly (Ed.) *Deviant Behavior* (pp. 181-199). New York: St. Martins.

Staples, R. (1993). *Black Families at the Crossroads: Challenges and Prospects.* San Francisco, CA: Jossey-Bass.

Stevens, S. (1993). HIV Prevention Programs in a Jail Setting: Educational Strategies. *The Prison Journal,* 73, 379-390.

Simon, H. (1957). *Models of Man, Social and Rational: Mathematical Essays on Rational Human Behavior in a Social Setting.* New York: Wiley.

Stinchcombe, A. (1990). *Information and Organizations.* Berkeley, CA: University of California Press.

Streetman, L. (2006). Health on the Inside, Health on the Outside: the Impact of Place on Inmates' Health. Paper presented at the Eastern Sociological Society annual meetings, Boston, MA.

Streetman, L. (2004a). Health Risks and Concerns among Released Offenders. Paper presented at the American Sociological Association annual meetings, San Francisco, CA.

Streetman, L. (2004b). Offender Community Transition: Re-establishing Family and Work Roles. Paper presented at the Eastern Sociological Society annual meetings, New York, NY.

Streetman, L. (2002). Incarceration-to-Community Transition: Local, National, Global HIV Risk. *Proceedings of the Ghana Conference, Global Awareness Society International*, X, 158-168.

Streetman, L. (1996). *Drugs, Delinquency, and Pregnancy, A Panel Study of Adolescent Problem Behaviors*. New York: Vantage.

Taxman, F., Young, D., and Byrne, J. (2002). Offender's Views of Reentry: Implications for Processes, Programs, and Services. College Park, MD: Bureau of Governmental Research.

Tillman, P. and Pequegnat, W. (1997). Interventions to Prevent HIV Risk Behaviors. *Current Bibliographies in Medicine*, National Library of Medicine: Bethesda, MD.

UNAIDS/WHO. (2006). "2006 Report on the Global AIDS Epidemic." www.UNAIDS.org.

Walmsley, R. (2006). "World Prison Population List." (6th ed.). www.prisonstudies.org.

Wray, L. and Stone, E. (2005). The role of self-esteem and anxiety in decision making for self versus others in relationships. *Journal of Behavioral Decision Making*, 18, 125-144.

Weber, E., Blais, A., and Betz, N. (2002). A domain-specific risk-attitude scale: measuring risk perceptions and risk behaviors. *Journal of Behavioral Decision Making*, 15, 263-290.

Williams, L. (2007). Warden to meeting: No interest in health care. *Wilmington News Journal*, Feb. 23: A1.

About the Author

Lee Streetman has a doctorate in sociology from the University of Delaware. A Vietnam-era Marine stationed overseas, he has tutored in juvenile and adult correctional facilities. He is researching his Cherokee heritage and is an avid civil war buff and amateur astronomer. Dr. Streetman is an Associate Professor at Delaware State University in Dover, where he teaches sociology and criminal justice.

Index

978-0-595-46001-4
0-595-46001-1